An Enemy of the People

Henrik Ibsen (1828-1906). Norwegian poet and play-wright. His plays include: *Peer Gynt* (1867), *A Doll's House* (1879), *Ghosts* (1881), *An Enemy of the People* (1882), *Hedda Gabler* (1890) and *The Master Builder* (1892).

Christopher Hampton was born in the Azores in 1946. He wrote his first play, *When Did You Last See My Mother?*, at the age of eighteen. His work for theatre, television and cinema includes *The Philanthropist*, translations of Yasmina Reza's *'Art'* and *The Unexpected Man*, his adaptation of *Les Liaisons Dangereuses* by Laclos, translations from Ibsen and Molière and the screenplays *Dangerous Liaisons*, *Carrington* and *The Secret Agent*.

HENRIK IBSEN

An Enemy of the People

in a new version by
Christopher Hampton

faber and faber
LONDON · BOSTON

First published in 1997
by Faber and Faber Limited
3 Queen Square London WC1N 3AU

Typeset by Faber and Faber Ltd
Printed in England by Mackays of Chatham plc, Chatham, Kent

A CIP record for this book
is available from the British Library

ISBN 0–571–19429–X

4 6 8 10 9 7 5

Introduction

For me, *An Enemy of the People* has always been an especially significant play, if only because, as far as I can recall, it was the first play I ever saw. It seems a slightly unlikely choice for an Egyptian school in the pre-Suez crisis fifties, and not necessarily calculated to stir the imagination of an eight-year-old already addicted to the Westerns, thrillers and CinemaScope epics of Hollywood; but it must have been a lively production in the Assembly Hall of the British Boys' School in Alexandria. It survives in my memory over forty years later as a series of vivid snapshots, like the moment when, to my intense confusion and subsequent delight, a planted heckler rose from his seat beside me to harangue and shout down the dignified figure of Dr Stockmann, trying to make himself heard from the stage. Recently, in an autobiographical play called *White Chameleon*, I attributed to this experience the birth of my serious interest in theatre; no doubt something of an oversimplification, but, at the very least, it was the first of a long series of occasions when I have been inspired and sustained by the rigorous, uncomfortable, but profoundly humane genius of Ibsen.

Chronologically, *An Enemy of the People* falls between two other masterpieces I have been fortunate enough to translate: *Ghosts* (1881) and *The Wild Duck* (1884); but before developing this thought, I should perhaps define what I mean by 'translate'. I do not speak Norwegian, but I am a trained linguist, accustomed to translating directly from French and German, which has enabled me to devise my own slightly eccentric method of tackling Ibsen. I work from the original text, with a Norwegian dictionary, supported by a literal translation prepared by a Norwegian speaker (in this case, Charlotte Barslund) and the original German translation. Ibsen spent a great deal of his time in Germany, where his plays were much performed, and kept a close eye on translations into the one foreign language he knew his way around (he had no English or French). The root similarities between German and Norwegian (Norwegian has been described as 'German spoken under-water') make German translations a useful bridge to the original text for the non-Norwegian speaker; and the bene-fits of working directly from the original text are consider-able. Ibsen used particular words or turns of phrase like Wagnerian leitmotifs (an obvious example is the word 'tøre' [to dare], used even more extensively here than it was to be in *Hedda Gabler* [1890], indicating how cen-trally both plays deal with failures of courage); and only a scrutiny of Ibsen's text can reveal how many speeches are interrupted or uncompleted, underlining his demand in a letter to the director of the Christiania Theatre for 'the greatest possible naturalism'. 'Above all,' he continued, 'truthfulness to nature – the illusion that everything is real and that one is sitting and watching something that is actually taking place in real life'; and it's this concern for realism which gives the play a roughness and speed (it only took Ibsen a year to write instead of his habitual two) which contrasts with the classical formality of *Ghosts* and the more complex and poetic textures of *The Wild Duck*.

Ibsen had expected *Ghosts*, his medically inaccurate but psychologically precise play about hereditary syphilis, to provoke a strong reaction ('*Ghosts* will probably cause alarm in some circles,' he wrote to his publisher, Frederik Hegel); but the storm of outraged protest which burst over his head was entirely unexpected in its vindictive frenzy. *An Enemy of the People* certainly has its origins in the feelings of righteous indignation which arose in Ibsen when *Ghosts* was condemned not only in the conservative press (which was inevitable) but also, and even more furiously, in the liberal press. So Dr Stockmann's contempt for the liberal majority was, for the moment, Ibsen's; and the idea of Dr Stockmann as the beleaguered individual courageously confronting a selfish and corrupt society has persisted, no doubt abetted by Arthur Miller's excellent adaptation of the play, which, pursuing its own agenda, portrayed Stockmann as a heroic bulwark against the as it were Macarthyite forces of mendacious self-interest.

This is to simplify Ibsen's intent; because however sympathetic Ibsen feels towards Dr Stockmann's cause, he is too subtle and profound a dramatist not to know that there are few figures more infuriating than the man who is always right. Stockmann's sincerity, naïvety and courage co-exist with an innocent vanity, an inability to compromise and an indifference to the havoc caused in the lives of his family and friends, as well as his own, by his dogged pursuit of principle. These latter elements, which round out the portrait of Dr Stockmann, were the very characteristics Ibsen was to pursue further in *The Wild Duck*, where the far less sympathetic, indeed dangerously self-righteous Gregers Werle descends on the Ekdal household, brandishing 'the demands of idealism', and succeeds in laying waste everything he claims to hold most dear.

It is this even-handedness and refusal to oversimplify that makes *An Enemy of the People* as powerfully relevant in our age of *fin-de-siècle* corruption, ecological vandalism and truculent refusal to accept inconvenient facts, as it was in pre-revolutionary Russia (where Dr Stockmann was one of Stanislavsky's most popular roles) or, for that matter, post-colonial Egypt. 'To write,' Ibsen famously said, 'is to sit in judgement on oneself'; a credo which lies at the root of his plays' perennial vitality and will always set him apart from the liberal majority of writers who are content merely to sit in judgement on other people.

Christopher Hampton
August 1997

Characters

Doctor Tomas Stockmann, Medical Officer at the Baths
Mrs Stockmann, his wife
Petra, their daughter, a teacher
Ejlif, their son, aged 13
Morten, their son, aged 10
Peter Stockmann, the doctor's elder brother, the mayor and
chief of police, Chairman of the Board at the Baths, etc.
Morten Kiil, a master tanner, Mrs Stockmann's foster-
father
Hovstad, editor of *The People's Messenger*
Billing, on the staff of the paper
Captain Horster
Aslaksen, a printer
The audience at a public meeting: men of every class, a
few women, a drunk and a gang of schoolboys

*The action of the play takes place in a town on the
southern coast of Norway.*

*The text printed here is as at the beginning of rehearsals
and does not include any of the changes, cuts, improvements or disimprovements which may have been made
during the course of production.*

An Enemy of the People was first performed at the Royal National Theatre's Olivier Theatre on 12 September 1997 with the following cast:

Doctor Tomas Stockmann Ian McKellen
Mrs Katrine Stockmann Penny Downie
Petra Stockmann Lucy Whybrow
Ejlif Stockmann Daniel Forster-Smith/Kai Pearce
Morten Stockmann Edward Brown/Robert Smithson
Peter Stockmann Stephen Moore
Morten Kiil Ralph Nossek
Hovstad Alan Cox
Billing Marston Bloom
Captain Horster Alisdair Simpson
Aslaksen John Woodvine
Randine Sally-Ann Burnett
Mr Vik Bryan Robson
Pettersen Seymour Matthews
Evensen Chris Gillespie
Lamstad Edward Clayton
Osvald Patrick Romer
Knudson Michael Mawby
Mrs Busk Naomi Capron
Engstrand Murray McArthur
Thoresen Robert Aldous
Stabell Guy Manning
Lammers Jim Creighton
Bjornson Alan Brown
Hansen Michael Haughey
Grimstad Alan White

Directed by Trevor Nunn
Designed by John Napier
Costumes by John Bright
Lighting by David Hersey
Music by Steven Edis

Act One

It's evening in the doctor's living-room, which is modestly but neatly furnished and decorated. There are two doors stage right, the further of which leads out to the hall, while the nearer opens into the doctor's study. Opposite the hall door is a door leading to the family's other rooms. A tiled stove stands in the middle of the wall and further downstage is a sofa above which is a mirror and in front of which is an oval table with a tablecloth. On the table is a lighted lamp with a shade. Upstage, an open door leads into the dining-room, where the table is laid and the lamp is lit.

Billing sits at the dinner-table, with a napkin tucked under his chin. Mrs Stockmann stands by the table, handing him a dish with a large joint of roast beef. The other seats around the table are empty and the place settings are in disarray, as at the end of a meal.

Mrs Stockmann Well, if you arrive an hour late, Mr Billing, you have to make do with cold.

Billing (*eating*) Tastes delicious . . . absolutely first rate.

Mrs Stockmann You know how fussy Stockmann is about having his meals on time . . .

Billing I don't mind a bit. That's when it tastes best, if you ask me, when you can sit on your own and concentrate on what you're eating.

Mrs Stockmann Good, as long as it tastes all right . . . (*She hears something in the hall.*) That must be Hovstad.

Billing Shouldn't wonder.

Mayor Peter Stockmann enters in his overcoat and official cap, carrying his stick.

Mayor A very good evening to you, Katrine.

Mrs Stockmann steps into the living-room.

Mrs Stockmann Ah, it's you, good evening. Kind of you to look in on us.

Mayor I was just passing and . . . (*He glances in the direction of the dining-room.*) Oh, but I see you already have company.

Mrs Stockmann (*slightly embarrassed*) No, not really; it's just a casual visit. (*hastily*) Won't you go in and have a little something?

Mayor Me? No thank you very much. Good heavens, a cooked meal in the evening, not with my digestive system.

Mrs Stockmann Go on, just this once . . .

Mayor No, no, thanks all the same; I'll stick to my tea and sandwiches. It's healthier in the long run . . . not to mention cheaper.

Mrs Stockmann (*smiling*) You mustn't think Tomas and I are extravagant.

Mayor Not you, Katrine; on the contrary. (*He points at the doctor's study.*) He's not in, by any chance?

Mrs Stockmann No, he's gone for a little after-dinner walk . . . with the boys.

Mayor Do you think that's good for him? (*listening*) There he is.

Mrs Stockmann No, that's not him.

There's a knock at the door.

Come in!

Hovstad enters from the hall.

Oh, it's you, Mr Hovstad . . .

Hovstad Yes, I'm sorry; I was held up down at the printing-works. Mr Mayor, good evening.

Mayor (*greeting him a little stiffly*) Mr Hovstad. I expect you're here on business, are you?

Hovstad Partly. There's an article.

Mayor I imagine. From what I hear, my brother's a pretty prolific contributor to *The People's Messenger*.

Hovstad Yes, he's not averse to writing for *The Messenger* when he feels that something needs saying.

Mrs Stockmann (*to Hovstad*) Would you like some . . .? (*She points in the direction of the dining-room.*)

Mayor Heavens, I certainly don't blame him if he wants to write for the class where he's most likely to find support. Besides which, Mr Hovstad, as far as your paper's concerned, I personally have no axe to grind.

Hovstad I should think not.

Mayor All in all, ours is a wonderfully tolerant community . . . really public-spirited. And the reason for that is that we're united by a great common cause . . . a cause which is of equal concern to every right-minded citizen . . .

Hovstad The Baths, you mean.

Mayor Exactly. Our great, new, magnificent Baths. You wait! Those Baths are going to be at the very centre of the life of this town, Mr Hovstad. No doubt about it.

Mrs Stockmann That's what Tomas says.

3

Mayor Think of the extraordinary improvements there have been, just in these last couple of years! People have a bit of money now; there's life and enterprise. Land and property values are going up every day.

Hovstad And unemployment's going down.

Mayor That as well, yes. There's been a very satisfying drop in the welfare payments our ratepayers have to meet, and things can only get better this year, provided we have a really good summer . . . a really big influx of visitors . . . we want those sick people pouring in, and the reputation of the Baths will be made.

Hovstad And there's every chance of that happening, I gather.

Mayor It's looking very promising. We're getting enquiries about accommodation and so on every day.

Hovstad Well, then, the doctor's article couldn't be more timely.

Mayor What's he written about this time?

Hovstad This is something he wrote last winter; recommending the Baths, underlining all the positive health implications. But I didn't run it at the time.

Mayor You mean there was some sort of catch in it?

Hovstad No, not at all; I just thought better to leave it till spring; now's the time people are starting to think about their summer holidays . . .

Mayor Quite right; absolutely right, Mr Hovstad.

Mrs Stockmann Yes, if it's anything to do with the Baths, Tomas is completely indefatigable.

Mayor Well, after all, that's his job.

Hovstad And they're his creation, aren't they, he's the only begetter.

Mayor Is he? Is that right? Yes, it's an opinion I've heard expressed from time to time. And yet I was under the impression I'd also played a modest part in this initiative.

Mrs Stockmann Yes, that's what Tomas always says.

Hovstad Nobody would deny that, Mr Mayor. You got it all up and running and dealt with the practicalities; everybody knows that. I just meant the original idea was the doctor's.

Mayor Yes, ideas, my brother's certainly had enough of them in his time . . . unfortunately. But when something actually needs to be done, a different sort of personality is called for, Mr Hovstad. And I did think, at least in this house . . .

Mrs Stockmann But, Peter . . .

Hovstad You can't possibly think . . .

Mrs Stockmann Go in and get yourself something to eat, Mr Hovstad; I'm sure my husband will be here soon.

Hovstad Thank you; perhaps just a bite. (*He goes into the dining-room.*)

Mayor (*lowering his voice a little*) It's a funny thing about people from peasant families: tact is something they never manage to acquire.

Mrs Stockmann It's hardly worth worrying about. You and Tomas are brothers, surely you can share the credit?

Mayor Yes, you'd have thought so; but not everyone's prepared to share, by the look of it.

Mrs Stockmann Nonsense! You and Tomas get on excep-

5

tionally well. (*listening*) I think that's him now. (*She goes over and opens the hall door.*)

Dr Stockmann (*laughing and speaking in a loud voice off-stage*) Look, I've brought you home another guest, Katrine. What fun, eh? Please, Captain Horster; hang your coat on the peg. Oh, you're not wearing a coat, are you? Guess what, Katrine, I nabbed him in the street; had to twist his arm to make him come up.

Captain Horster enters and greets Mrs Stockmann.

(*in the doorway*) In you go, boys. Course, they're starving again! Come along, Captain Horster; you're going to taste a piece of beef that'll . . .

He's herding Horster into the dining-room. Ejlif and Morten follow him in.

Mrs Stockmann But, Tomas, haven't you noticed . . .?

Dr Stockmann turns in the doorway.

Dr Stockmann Ah, Peter, it's you! (*He goes over to shake hands with him.*) Well, this is fun.

Mayor I'm afraid I've only got a minute . . .

Dr Stockmann Never heard such nonsense; there'll be hot toddy on the table soon. You haven't forgotten the toddy, have you, Katrine?

Mrs Stockmann Course not; the water's just boiling. (*She goes into the dining-room.*)

Mayor Hot toddy as well . . .!

Dr Stockmann Yes, go on, sit down, let's make ourselves comfortable.

Mayor No thank you; I'm not much of a one for drinking parties.

Dr Stockmann This isn't what I call a party.

Mayor Looks like one to me. (*He takes a look at the dining-room.*) Amazing the amount of food they manage to put away.

Dr Stockmann (*rubbing his hands*) Yes, it's wonderful watching young people eat, isn't it? Perpetual appetite, mm? Just as it should be. They must have food! Energy! These are the people whose job it'll be to ginger up the bubbling soup of the future, Peter.

Mayor Dare I ask what sort of thing might need 'gingering up', as you put it?

Dr Stockmann Oh, you'll have to ask the youngsters about that . . . when the time comes. Naturally we wouldn't understand. Obviously. Two old buffers like you and me . . .

Mayor Steady on! That's a very extreme expression . . .

Dr Stockmann Now, you don't have to take me so literally, Peter. I must tell you, I'm genuinely pleased and happy. I feel I'm so indescribably fortunate to be surrounded by all this burgeoning, exploding life. These are glorious times to be alive! It's as if a whole new world was coming into existence.

Mayor Do you really think so?

Dr Stockmann Well, of course, you can't see it as clearly as I can. You've lived here all your life; and that blunts your perceptions. But I spent all those many years stuck up north in that out-of-the-way hole, hardly ever setting eyes on an outsider, or anyone who might have had something stimulating to say . . . so the effect on me is as if I'd been dropped into the centre of some teeming metropolis . . .

Mayor Metropolis, eh . . .?

Dr Stockmann Yes, naturally I know this is small scale compared to lots of other towns. But there is life here . . . promise, a whole variety of things worth working for and fighting for; and that's the main thing. (*shouting*) Katrine, has the postman been?

Mrs Stockmann (*from the dining-room*) No, nobody's been.

Dr Stockmann And then there's making a good living, Peter! That's something you learn to appreciate when you've been teetering on the brink of starvation, the way we have . . .

Mayor Good heavens . . .

Dr Stockmann Oh, yes, things were pretty tight up there, often, as I'm sure you can imagine. And now we can live like princes! Today, for example, we had roast beef for lunch; and we had it for dinner as well. Wouldn't you like to taste a bit? Or at least let me show it to you? Come . . .

Mayor No, no, really . . .

Dr Stockmann Oh, come on. Look, we've got a table-cloth.

Mayor Yes, so I noticed.

Dr Stockmann And we have a lampshade as well. See? All out of Katrine's savings. Makes the room so comfort-able. Don't you think? Stand over here . . . no, no, no, not there. Here; that's right. You see; how it sort of directs the light downwards . . . I think it looks really elegant. Don't you?

Mayor Yes, if you can indulge yourself in such luxuries . . .

Dr Stockmann Oh, yes, I think I can indulge myself now. Katrine tells me I'm earning nearly as much as we spend.

Mayor Nearly as much, I see . . .!

Dr Stockmann Well, a scientist ought to live in some sort of style. I'm sure an ordinary magistrate spends far more a year than I do.

Mayor Well, so I should think! A magistrate, a senior public official . . .

Dr Stockmann All right then, say, a simple wholesale dealer! Someone like that would spend three times as much as . . .

Mayor That's the way things are.

Dr Stockmann Not that I waste anything on frivolities, Peter. But I just don't think I can deny myself the pleasure of seeing people in my house. It's something I need, you see. I've been out of touch for so long . . . it's a vital necessity for me to spend time with young, outspoken, lively people, free-thinking people, doers . . . and that's what they are, every one of them sitting enjoying their food in there. I wish you knew Hovstad a little better . . .

Mayor Yes, Hovstad, that's right, he was telling me he wants to publish another one of your articles.

Dr Stockmann An article of mine?

Mayor Yes, about the Baths. Some article you wrote last winter.

Dr Stockmann Oh, that, yes! . . . No, I don't want that published just now.

Mayor You don't? I would have thought that now would be precisely the right time.

Dr Stockmann Yes, under normal circumstances you might be right . . .

He crosses the room. The mayor is watching him.

Mayor Are the circumstances abnormal?

Dr Stockmann (*stopping*) Well, Peter, I can't really explain it to you at the moment; not tonight anyway. Maybe there are a good many abnormal circumstances; and maybe there aren't. Maybe it's all in my imagination.

Mayor That sounds very mysterious, I must say. Is there something the matter? Something being kept from me? I would have thought as Chairman of the Board at the Baths, I'm . . .

Dr Stockmann And I would have thought that I, as . . . well, don't let's go for each other's jugular, Peter.

Mayor Good Lord, I'm not in the habit of going for the jugular, as you put it. But I must absolutely insist that all decisions must be considered and implemented in a businesslike manner by the legally constituted authorities. I cannot permit anything crooked or underhand.

Dr Stockmann Have you ever known me to be connected with anything crooked or underhand?

Mayor There's no doubt you have a deep-rooted tendency to go your own way. And in a well-ordered community, that's almost as undesirable. The individual has to learn to submit to society, or, more accurately, to submit to the authorities whose job it is to decide what's good for society.

Dr Stockmann Quite possibly. But what the hell's that got to do with me?

Mayor My dear Tomas, that's exactly what you never seem to be prepared to learn. You take my word for it: one of these days you're going to have to pay for that . . . sooner or later. Now I've said it. Goodbye.

Dr Stockmann Have you gone mad? You're barking up

completely the wrong tree . . .

Mayor That's not something I do. In any case I'm not going to put up with your . . . (*turning to the dining-room*) Goodbye, Katrine. Goodbye, gentlemen.

He exits. Mrs Stockmann steps into the living-room.

Mrs Stockmann Has he gone?

Dr Stockmann Yes, in a filthy temper.

Mrs Stockmann Oh, Tomas, darling, what have you done to him this time?

Dr Stockmann Nothing at all. He can't demand I give him information before the time is right.

Mrs Stockmann What information are you supposed to have given him?

Dr Stockmann Well: leave that to me, Katrine . . . It's strange, the postman hasn't been.

Hovstad, Billing and Horster have got up from the table and come into the living-room. Ejlif and Morten follow a bit later. Billing stretches out his arms.

Billing I'll be damned if a meal like that doesn't make you feel like a new man.

Hovstad The mayor wasn't very cheery this evening.

Dr Stockmann It's his stomach; he has trouble with his digestion.

Hovstad He particularly has trouble digesting anyone who works for *The People's Messenger*.

Mrs Stockmann You seemed to be getting on all right.

Hovstad Yes, a kind of armistice, nothing more.

Billing That's exactly right. The *mot juste*.

Dr Stockmann We have to remember that Peter's a lonely man, poor fellow. There's nothing for him at home, nowhere he can unwind; everything's just business and more business. And all that damned weak tea he keeps swilling. All right, boys, pull the chairs up to the table! Katrine, let's have the hot toddy.

Mrs Stockmann sets off towards the dining-room.

Mrs Stockmann It's on its way.

Dr Stockmann And you sit here on the sofa with me, Captain Horster. We hardly ever see you . . . Please sit down, my friends.

They sit down round the table. Mrs Stockmann brings a tray, with a kettle, glasses, decanters and so on.

Mrs Stockmann Now: this is arrack and this one is rum; and here's the brandy. Everyone help themselves.

Dr Stockmann (*taking a glass*) We certainly shall. (*as the toddy is being stirred*) Fetch the cigars out, Ejlif, you know where they live. And you, Morten, you can bring me my pipe.

The boys go into the room, stage right.

I suspect Ejlif pinches a cigar every so often; but I turn a blind eye. (*shouting*) And my cap, Morten! Katrine, can you tell him where I left it? Oh, he's found it!

The boys come back with what's required.

Please, my friends. Personally, I stick to my pipe; this one's been on a good many stormy passages with me up there in the north. (*clinking his glass*) Cheers! It's so much better sitting down here safe and sound.

Mrs Stockmann (*sitting down, knitting*) Are you sailing soon, Captain Horster?

Horster I should be ready next week.

Mrs Stockmann And will you be going to America?

Horster That's the idea.

Billing You're going to miss the next council election.

Horster Is there going to be an election?

Billing Didn't you know?

Horster No, I don't get involved in that sort of thing.

Billing Surely you take an interest in public issues.

Horster No, I don't really understand them.

Billing All the same; you ought to vote.

Horster Even if you don't understand?

Billing Understand? What are you talking about? Society is like a ship; you need all hands to the rudder.

Horster Maybe on land; wouldn't get you very far on board ship.

Hovstad Strange how little most sailors care about what happens in their home country.

Billing Quite extraordinary.

Dr Stockmann Sailors are birds of passage; north or south, they feel at home. That's why all the rest of us must be all the more active, Mr Hovstad. Anything to the point in *The Messenger* tomorrow?

Hovstad Nothing about local politics. But the day after tomorrow, I was thinking of running your article . . .

Dr Stockmann Oh, God, yes, my article! No, listen, you'll have to delay that.

Hovstad Really? We have plenty of space and I thought

this was probably the most telling moment to . . .

Dr Stockmann Yes, yes, you may be right; but you'll have to wait, all the same. I'll explain later . . .

Petra comes in from the hall in her hat and cloak, a number of exercise books under her arm.

Petra Good evening.

Dr Stockmann Is that you, Petra? Good evening.

General salutations. Petra puts her outdoor clothes and books on a chair by the door.

Petra So here you all are lazing about, while I've been out slaving away.

Dr Stockmann Well, come in and laze about with us.

Billing May I mix you a little drink?

Petra comes over to the table.

Petra No thanks, better if I do it myself; you always make it too strong. By the way, father, I have a letter for you. (*She goes over to the chair, where her clothes are.*)

Dr Stockmann A letter? From whom?

Petra is searching in the pocket of her cloak.

Petra The postman handed it to me just as I was on my way out . . .

Dr Stockmann gets up and goes over to her.

Dr Stockmann And you wait till now to bring it to me!

Petra I really didn't have time to run back up. So, here it is.

Dr Stockmann grabs the letter.

Dr Stockmann Let's have a look; let's have a look, dear.

(*He checks the signature.*) Yes, this is it . . .!

Mrs Stockmann Is that what you've been waiting for, Tomas?

Dr Stockmann Certainly is; I must go straight in and . . . Where do I find some light, Katrine? Don't tell me there's no lamp in my study again!

Mrs Stockmann Yes, the lamp's lit and sitting on your desk.

Dr Stockmann Good, good. Excuse me a minute . . . (*He goes into his study, stage right.*)

Petra What's all this about, mother?

Mrs Stockmann No idea; in the last couple of days he's kept asking about the postman.

Billing Probably some patient out in the country . . .

Petra Poor father; before long he's going to be overworked again. (*She mixes herself a drink.*) Ah, I'm looking forward to this.

Hovstad Have you been teaching evening classes today as well?

Petra (*sipping her drink*) Two hours.

Billing And four hours this morning at the institute . . .

Petra (*sitting at the table*) Five hours.

Mrs Stockmann And I see you have books to mark this evening.

Petra Yes, a huge pile.

Horster You keep yourself busy, by the look of it.

Petra Yes, but I like it. Means you get delightfully tired.

Billing Is that good?

Petra Yes, then you sleep like a log.

Morten You must be a real sinner, Petra.

Petra A sinner?

Morten Yes, because you work so hard. Mr Rørlund says work's a punishment for your sins.

Ejlif (*contemptuously*) Huh, you must be stupid if that's what you think.

Mrs Stockmann Now, now, Ejlif.

Billing (*laughing*) No, that's very good.

Hovstad Wouldn't you like to work hard, Morten?

Morten No, I would not.

Hovstad Well, what do you want to do when you grow up?

Morten I want to be a Viking.

Ejlif But then you can't be a Christian.

Morten I don't care.

Billing I'm on your side, Morten! That's exactly what I say.

Mrs Stockmann (*making signs at him*) No, you don't, Mr Billing, I'm sure you don't.

Billing I bloody well do . . .! I'm not a Christian and I'm proud of it. You wait, soon there won't be any Christians.

Morten And then can we do whatever we like?

Billing Well, Morten, the thing is . . .

Mrs Stockmann Off you go, boys; I'm sure you have

some homework to do for tomorrow.

Ejlif I can stay a bit longer, can't I . . .?

Mrs Stockmann No, you can't; go on, both of you.

The boys say goodnight and go off through the door, stage left.

Hovstad Do you really think this sort of talk can do the boys any harm?

Mrs Stockmann Well, I don't know; but I don't like it.

Petra I think you're wrong, mother.

Mrs Stockmann It's possible; but I don't like it; not here at home.

Petra There are so many lies, at home and at school. At home you're supposed to keep quiet, and at school you have to stand up in front of the children and tell lies.

Hovstad You have to tell lies?

Petra Well, you can imagine, we have to teach them a good many things we don't believe ourselves.

Billing Yes, I'm sure you do.

Petra If I could afford it, I'd set up a school myself and run things quite differently.

Billing Oh, afford it . . .

Horster Well, if that's what you want, Miss Stockmann, you're welcome to have some rooms in my house. Since my father died, his enormous old house has been almost empty; there's a very big dining-room downstairs . . .

Petra (*laughing*) Yes, well, thank you; but it isn't going to happen.

Hovstad No, I think Miss Petra would rather take up journalism. Which reminds me, have you had time to take a look at that English story you promised to translate for us?

Petra No, not yet; but you'll get it in good time.

Dr Stockmann enters from his study, the opened letter in his hand.

Dr Stockmann (*flourishing the letter*) Here's some news that'll raise a few questions in the town, you take my word for it!

Billing News?

Mrs Stockmann What sort of news?

Dr Stockmann A major discovery, Katrine!

Hovstad Really?

Mrs Stockmann Made by you?

Dr Stockmann Absolutely made by me. (*pacing up and down*) Now let them try their usual trick and claim it's a brainstorm or some lunatic stunt. They'd better watch out this time! Ha ha, yes, they'd better watch out!

Petra Are you going to tell us what it is, father?

Dr Stockmann Oh, yes; just give me time, all will be revealed. If only Peter were here now! This just goes to show our human tendency to run around passing judgement when we're as reliable as a lot of blind moles . . .

Hovstad What do you mean, Doctor?

Dr Stockmann (*stopping by the table*) Is it not the general opinion that our town is a healthy place?

Hovstad Yes, everyone knows that.

Dr Stockmann More than that, a quite exceptionally healthy place . . . a place which deserves to be very warmly recommended to everyone, sick or well . . .

Mrs Stockmann Tomas, darling . . .

Dr Stockmann And we have recommended it and praised it to the skies. I've written and written, pamphlets and articles in *The Messenger*.

Hovstad Yes, well, so?

Dr Stockmann These Baths, which have been called the town's arteries and the town's central nervous system and . . . and God knows what else . . .

Billing 'The town's beating heart' I once called them in an extravagant moment . . .

Dr Stockmann Yes, quite. But do you know what they really are, our great, magnificent, acclaimed Baths, which cost such a fortune . . . do you know what they are?

Hovstad No, what are they?

Mrs Stockmann What are they?

Dr Stockmann Those Baths are a sink of disease.

Petra The Baths, father?

Mrs Stockmann (*simultaneously*) Our Baths!

Hovstad (*likewise*) But, Doctor . . .

Billing Quite incredible!

Dr Stockmann I'm telling you, those Baths are poisoned, they're a whited sepulchre. They're a tremendous health risk! All that muck up there in the valley where the mills are . . . all that stuff that smells so disgusting . . . it's infecting the water in the feed-pipes to the pump room; and the same damned poisonous filth is also leaking out on to the beach . . .

19

Horster You mean into the Sea Baths?

Dr Stockmann Exactly.

Hovstad How can you be so sure, Doctor?

Dr Stockmann I've made the most conscientious investigation possible. Oh, I've had my suspicions for a long time. Last year there were a number of unusual illnesses among the visitors to the Baths . . . typhus, gastric conditions . . .

Mrs Stockmann Yes, that's right.

Dr Stockmann At the time we thought the tourists had brought the infections with them; but later on . . . in the winter . . . I began to think differently; and then I started to analyse the water as best I could.

Mrs Stockmann So that's what you've been so busy doing!

Dr Stockmann I've been busy, Katrine, you can say that again. But I didn't have the scientific instruments I needed; so I sent specimens of both the drinking water and the sea water to the university laboratory to get a precise chemical analysis.

Hovstad And that's what you just received?

Dr Stockmann (*brandishing the letter*) This is it! This proves that decomposing organic matter is present in the water . . . vast quantities of bacteria. It would have a disastrous effect on health, whether taken internally or externally.

Mrs Stockmann What a blessing you discovered this in time.

Dr Stockmann Absolutely.

Hovstad And now what do you intend to do, Doctor?

Dr Stockmann Put things right, of course.

Hovstad Can that be done?

Dr Stockmann It has to be done. Otherwise the Baths are completely unusable . . . finished. But there's no danger of that. I'm quite clear about what measures need to be taken.

Mrs Stockmann You've kept all this such a secret, Tomas dear.

Dr Stockmann I suppose I should have run round town telling everyone, before I knew for certain? No, thanks; I'm not that stupid.

Petra You could have told us . . .

Dr Stockmann Not a living soul. But tomorrow you can run up and tell old Badger . . .

Mrs Stockmann Tomas, really . . .!

Dr Stockmann All right, you can tell your grandfather. That'll give the old boy something to chew over; he thinks I'm soft in the head; and a good many people feel that way, as I'm very well aware. Well, this'll show them, all those worthies . . . this'll really show them . . .! (*pacing up and down, rubbing his hands*) There's going to be such a hoo-ha in town, Katrine! You can't imagine. The entire water supply is going to have to be relaid.

Hovstad (*getting up*) The entire water supply . . .?

Dr Stockmann Well, of course it is. The intake is too low down; it needs to be moved higher up the hill.

Petra So you were right all along.

Dr Stockmann Yes, you remember, Petra: I wrote and complained before they started building. But nobody took a blind bit of notice. Well, now I'm going to give them both barrels . . . that's right; of course, I've written a report for the Board; I had it ready a week ago; I was just waiting for this. (*flourishing the letter*) I'm sending it off right away. (*He goes into his study and returns with a sheaf of papers.*) Look at this! Five whole pages, single-spaced! And a covering letter. Get me a newspaper, Katrine! Something to wrap it up in. Good; there we are; give it to . . . you know . . . (*stamping his foot*) What the hell's her name? The maid, give it to her; tell her it's to go straight to the mayor.

> *Mrs Stockmann takes the parcel and exits through the dining-room.*

Petra What do you think uncle Peter's going to say, father?

Dr Stockmann What can he say? All I do know is that he'll certainly be pleased such a vital fact has come to light.

Hovstad Might I be allowed to publish a short piece on your discovery in *The Messenger*?

Dr Stockmann Yes, thank you, please do.

Hovstad I think it's advisable the public finds out about this sooner rather than later.

Dr Stockmann No doubt about it.

Mrs Stockmann (*returning*) She's taken it.

Billing God damn it, Doctor, you'll be the most important man in town.

Dr Stockmann (*pleased, moving around*) Oh, nonsense; basically all I've done is my duty. I've been lucky, I've dug up some buried treasure; nothing else. All the same . . .

Billing Hovstad, don't you think the town should lay on a torchlight parade for Doctor Stockmann?

Hovstad I'll arrange it.

Billing And I'll talk to Aslaksen about it.

Dr Stockmann My dear friends, let's not do anything silly; I don't want anybody making a fuss. And if the Board takes it into their heads to offer me a salary increase, I shan't accept it. I'm telling you, Katrine . . . I shan't accept it.

Mrs Stockmann Quite right, Tomas.

Petra (*raising her glass*) Cheers, father!

Hovstad and Billing Cheers, Doctor, cheers!

Horster (*clinking glasses with the doctor*) I hope this brings you nothing but good fortune.

Dr Stockmann Thank you, thank you, my dear friends! I couldn't be happier . . . oh, it's a blessing to know deep down that you've been of service to your home town and your fellow-citizens. Three cheers, Katrine!

> *He puts both hands behind her neck and spins her round and round. Mrs Stockmann shrieks and struggles. There's laughter, applause and cheers for the doctor. The boys put their heads round the door.*

Act Two

The living-room in the doctor's house. The door to the dining-room is closed. Morning.

   Mrs Stockmann enters from the dining-room with a letter in her hand, goes over to the door downstage right and peeps in.

Mrs Stockmann Are you back, Tomas?

Dr Stockmann (*off-stage*) Yes, I just came in. (*He enters.*) What is it?

Mrs Stockmann A letter from your brother. (*She hands it to him.*)

Dr Stockmann Aha, let's have a look. (*opening the letter and reading*) 'I'm returning the manuscript you sent me' . . . (*continuing to read, mumbling to himself*) Hm . . .

Mrs Stockmann What's he say?

   Dr Stockmann stuffs the letter into his pocket.

Dr Stockmann He just says he's coming up here around noon.

Mrs Stockmann You'd better remember to be here this time.

Dr Stockmann Well, I will; I've finished my morning rounds.

Mrs Stockmann I'm really curious to know how he's going to take it.

Dr Stockmann You wait, he's not going to be very happy

24

this discovery was made by me rather than him.

Mrs Stockmann Are you really worried about that?

Dr Stockmann No, you know, basically, he's going to be pleased about this. All the same . . . Peter gets so damned scared if he thinks anyone else apart from him is likely to make some contribution to the good of the town.

Mrs Stockmann Then, what about this, Tomas . . . why don't you be kind to him and let him share the credit? Couldn't you say it was him who put you on the right track . . .?

Dr Stockmann Fine, as far as I'm concerned. As long as I get it put right, I . . .

Old Morten Kiil puts his head around the hall door, looks around inquiringly.

Morten Kiil (*chuckles to himself and asks slyly*) Is this . . . is this true?

Mrs Stockmann (*turning to him*) Father . . . it's you!

Dr Stockmann Ah, Mr Kiil; good morning, good morning!

Mrs Stockmann Well, come in.

Morten Kiil Only if it's true; otherwise I'm off.

Dr Stockmann If what's true?

Morten Kiil This rubbish about the water supply. Is it true or isn't it?

Dr Stockmann Of course it's true. But how did you hear about it?

Morten Kiil (*coming in*) Petra popped in on her way to school . . .

Dr Stockmann Oh, did she?

Morten Kiil Yes; and then she told me . . . I thought she was pulling my leg; but that's not like Petra.

Dr Stockmann Really, how could you think that?

Morten Kiil Oh, you should never trust anyone; they'll make a fool of you before you know what's hit you. So it is true, after all?

Dr Stockmann Yes, I guarantee it. Won't you sit down, Mr Kiil? (*He persuades him to sit on the sofa.*) It's a real stroke of luck for the town, don't you think . . .?

Morten Kiil (*trying not to laugh*) A stroke of luck?

Dr Stockmann Yes, that I made this discovery in time . . .

Morten Kiil (*as before*) Oh, yes, yes! . . . But I never thought you'd pull these monkey tricks on your own brother.

Dr Stockmann Monkey tricks!

Mrs Stockmann Really, father . . .

Morten Kiil rests his hands and his chin on the knob of his stick and winks slyly at the doctor.

Morten Kiil What was it again? Something about animals getting into the water pipes?

Dr Stockmann Ah, yes, bacteria.

Morten Kiil And according to Petra, quite a lot of these animals had got in. Enormous numbers.

Dr Stockmann Well, yes; hundreds of thousands.

Morten Kiil But no one can see them, is that right?

Dr Stockmann No, you can't see them.

Morten Kiil (*quiet laughter bubbling*) Well, I'll be damned, this is the best one you've come up with yet.

26

Dr Stockmann What do you mean?

Morten Kiil You'll never get the mayor to believe that one, not in a thousand years.

Dr Stockmann Well, we'll see about that.

Morten Kiil You think he's that stupid?

Dr Stockmann I hope the whole town's that stupid.

Morten Kiil The whole town! Yes, well, so it might be. And serve them right; that'd teach them. Think they're so much cleverer than their elders. They hounded me out of the council. That's right; hounded me out, they did. And now it's their turn. So you pull your monkey tricks on them, Stockmann.

Dr Stockmann But, Mr Kiil . . .

Morten Kiil Pull your monkey tricks, I say. (*getting up*) And the mayor and his cronies, if you can put their noses out of joint, I'll go straight down and donate a hundred kroner to the poor.

Dr Stockmann Well, that's very handsome of you.

Morten Kiil I don't have a lot to throw around, as you know; but if you succeed, I'm going to donate fifty kroner to the poor on Christmas Eve.

Hovstad comes in from the hall.

Hovstad Good morning! (*coming to a halt*) Oh, I'm sorry . . .

Dr Stockmann No, come in; come in.

Morten Kiil (*chuckling again*) Him! Is he in on it as well?

Hovstad What do you mean?

Dr Stockmann Of course he's in on it.

Morten Kiil I can hardly believe it! It's going to be in the papers. You really are a one, Stockmann. Well, I'm off now; I'll leave you to your plotting.

Dr Stockmann No, stay a while, Mr Kiil.

Morten Kiil No, I'm off. And you think up as many monkey tricks as you can; it'll be worth your while, I can tell you.

He exits. Mrs Stockmann follows him out.

Dr Stockmann (*laughing*) What about that? . . . the old man thinks I made it all up about the water supply.

Hovstad Oh, that's what he was . . .

Dr Stockmann Yes, that's what we were talking about. And perhaps that's why you're here?

Hovstad That's right. Do you have a moment, Doctor?

Dr Stockmann My dear fellow, as long as you like.

Hovstad Have you heard from the mayor?

Dr Stockmann Not yet. He's coming here later.

Hovstad I've thought a great deal about this since last night.

Dr Stockmann And?

Hovstad You're a doctor and a scientist, for you this business with the water supply is something self-contained. I mean, it hasn't occurred to you that this is just part of a whole complex of issues.

Dr Stockmann In what way . . .? Let's sit down, old chap . . . No, take the sofa.

Hovstad sits on the sofa, the doctor in an armchair the other side of the table.

Now: what is it you mean?

Hovstad You said yesterday that the water pollution comes from impurities in the soil.

Dr Stockmann Yes, there's no doubt whatsoever it comes from that poisoned swamp in the valley where the mills are.

Hovstad I'm sorry, Doctor, I think it comes from a quite different sort of swamp.

Dr Stockmann What do you mean, what swamp?

Hovstad The swamp where the whole of our public life lies rotting.

Dr Stockmann What the hell are you talking about, Mr Hovstad?

Hovstad Little by little, everything in this town has fallen into the hands of a gang of bureaucrats . . .

Dr Stockmann Now, they're not all bureaucrats.

Hovstad No, but those of them who aren't actually bureaucrats are friends and supporters of bureaucrats; they're the rich or the old established names in the town; the ones who run everything and lord it over us.

Dr Stockmann Yes, but they're all people of ability and intelligence.

Hovstad How much ability and intelligence did they show when they laid the water pipes?

Dr Stockmann Well, obviously that was very stupid of them. But now it'll all be put right.

Hovstad How smooth a process do you think that'll be?

Dr Stockmann Smooth or not smooth . . . it's still going to happen.

Hovstad Yes, if the press comes in hard.

Dr Stockmann My dear old thing, that won't be necessary. I'm convinced my brother will . . .

Hovstad Forgive me, Doctor, but I'm telling you, I intend to deal with this matter.

Dr Stockmann In the paper?

Hovstad Yes. When I took over *The People's Messenger*, I was determined to explode this ring of opinionated old stuffed shirts who hold all the power.

Dr Stockmann But you told me yourself how that turned out: you almost ruined the paper.

Hovstad Yes, and then we had to step carefully for a while, it's true. Because if those men had been brought down, there was a danger the Baths would never have got the go-ahead. But now they're built, and we can do without the great and the good.

Dr Stockmann Perhaps we can do without them; but we owe them a great debt.

Hovstad They'll get their fair share of recognition. But a journalist with a reputation for radicalism, like myself, can't afford to let an opportunity like this slip away. I have to puncture the myth of the infallibility of the authorities. It has to be rooted out like any other superstition.

Dr Stockmann I wholeheartedly agree with you, Mr Hovstad; away with all superstition!

Hovstad I'm very loath to attack the mayor, because he's your brother. But I'm sure you agree with me that the truth outweighs all other considerations.

Dr Stockmann Yes, of course . . . (*involuntarily*) All the same . . .! All the same . . .!

Hovstad Don't think badly of me. I'm no more selfish or ambitious than the next man.

Dr Stockmann My dear fellow . . . who said you were?

Hovstad I come from a poor family, as you know; and I've had a first-hand opportunity to identify the worst deprivation of the lower classes. It's that they can take no part in controlling public affairs, Doctor. That's what develops ability and intelligence and self-respect . . .

Dr Stockmann I completely understand that . . .

Hovstad Yes . . . and I think if a journalist passes up a golden chance to bring freedom to the many, to the little people, to the oppressed, he's shouldering a heavy responsibility. I know very well . . . in the seats of power they'll call it subversion and I don't know what; but they can say what they like. As long as my conscience is clear, I . . .

Dr Stockmann Well, exactly! My dear Mr Hovstad, exactly. But even so . . . oh, damn it, I don't know . . .!

There's a knock at the door.

Come in!

The printer, Aslaksen, appears in the doorway to the hall. He's modestly but respectably dressed in black, with a slightly creased white cravat, carrying a top-hat and gloves.

Aslaksen (*bowing*) Please excuse me, Doctor, for taking the liberty of . . .

Dr Stockmann (*getting up*) Well, well . . . it's Mr Aslaksen!

Aslaksen That's right, Doctor.

Hovstad (*standing up*) Are you looking for me, Aslaksen?

Aslaksen No, I'm not; I didn't know I'd find you here. No, it was the doctor I . . .

Dr Stockmann Well, what can I do for you?

Aslaksen Is what I heard from Mr Billing true, that you're thinking of improving the water supply?

Dr Stockmann Yes, for the Baths.

Aslaksen Yes, that's what I thought. Well, I've come to tell you, you have my full support.

Hovstad (*to the doctor*) You see!

Dr Stockmann Well, I'm extremely grateful; but . . .

Aslaksen I think you might be glad to have us tradesmen behind you. Here in the town we constitute what you might call a solid majority . . . when we really *want* to. And it's always a good idea to have the majority behind you, Doctor.

Dr Stockmann I'm sure you're right; but I can scarcely foresee this requiring any particular effort. Seems to me a very clear and straightforward business.

Aslaksen All the same, it mightn't be a bad thing; I know our local authorities pretty well; there's one thing those in charge don't take very kindly to, and that's a suggestion from an outsider. That's why I think it wouldn't be out of order if we was to mount a little demonstration.

Hovstad Quite right, yes.

Dr Stockmann A demonstration, you say? What sort of a demonstration?

Aslaksen Something very moderate, Doctor, obviously; I'm very much in favour of moderation; moderation is the principal civic virtue . . . in my opinion, anyway.

Dr Stockmann You're well known for it, Mr Aslaksen.

Aslaksen Yes, I daresay I am. And this business with the water supply is something very important to us trades-men. The Baths look as if they might turn out to be a little gold mine for this town. We shall all be making our living from those Baths, especially us property-owners. So obvi-ously we want to give the Baths the strongest support we can. And since I'm the Chairman of the Property-owners' Association . . .

Dr Stockmann Go on . . .

Aslaksen . . . and since I'm also very active in the Temperance Society . . . well, I expect you know, Doctor, I do a lot of Temperance work?

Dr Stockmann Yes, so I gather.

Aslaksen Well . . . then you'll understand when I tell you I come into contact with a very broad spectrum. And as I'm known to be a responsible and law-abiding citizen, as you were kind enough to say yourself, I do have a certain influence in the town . . . a modest position of power . . . if I say so myself.

Dr Stockmann I'm very well aware of that, Mr Aslaksen.

Aslaksen Yes, you see . . . so it would be an easy matter for me to prepare a speech if that would suit.

Dr Stockmann A speech, you say?

Aslaksen Yes, a kind of speech on behalf of the citizens of this town, thanking you for having taken up this cause, which is so important to our community. Obviously, it would have to be phrased with suitable moderation, so as not to upset the authorities or people with influence. As long as we take that into careful consideration, I don't think anyone would be able to take offence, do you?

33

Hovstad Well, even if they don't like it very much, it's . . .

Aslaksen No, no, no; no outspokenness against the powers-that-be, Mr Hovstad. No outright opposition against people who are so intimately involved in our lives. I've seen enough of that in my time; and nothing good ever comes of it. But no citizen should be denied the right to express himself frankly and responsibly.

Dr Stockmann (*shaking his head*) My dear Mr Aslaksen, I can't tell you how delighted I am to find my fellow-citizens so sympathetic. I'm so pleased . . . so pleased! Listen; would you like a little glass of sherry? Mm?

Aslaksen No, thank you very much; I never touch spirits.

Dr Stockmann Well, then, a glass of beer; what do you think?

Aslaksen No, thank you, Doctor; I don't touch anything so early in the day. I'm going to pay a few visits in town and talk to some of the property-owners and start preparing the ground.

Dr Stockmann Well, it's extremely kind of you, Mr Aslaksen; but I still can't get it into my head that all these precautions should be necessary; I'm sure things will sort themselves out.

Aslaksen The workings of the authorities are very laborious, Doctor. And I don't say that to criticize, no, God forbid . . .

Hovstad We'll give them a jolt in the paper tomorrow, Aslaksen.

Aslaksen Nothing too violent, Mr Hovstad. Proceed with moderation, or you'll never budge them; my advice is worth listening to; I'm a graduate of the university of life . . . Well, I'll say goodbye, Doctor. Now you know, we tradesmen are behind you like a wall. The solid majority is on your side, Doctor.

Dr Stockmann Well, thank you, my dear Mr Aslaksen. (*shaking his hand*) Goodbye, goodbye!

Aslaksen Are you coming down to the press with me, Mr Hovstad?

Hovstad I'll be down soon; I have one or two decisions to make.

Aslaksen Fine, fine.

He bows and exits; Dr Stockmann follows him out into the hall.

Hovstad (*as the doctor returns*) Well, now what do you say, Doctor? Don't you think it's time to let in some air and put a rocket under all this inertia and apathy and cowardice?

Dr Stockmann Are you referring to Aslaksen?

Hovstad Yes, I am. He's one of those swamp-dwellers . . . however decent a man he may be. And most people round here are like that; they vacillate and veer from one side to the other; they have so many doubts and scruples, they're rooted to the spot.

Dr Stockmann Yes, but I think Aslaksen's very well meaning.

Hovstad There's something more important than that, in my opinion; to take a principled and confident stand.

Dr Stockmann I couldn't agree more.

Hovstad That's why I want to grasp this opportunity to try to put some backbone into the well meaning. This worship of authority that goes on here, it has to be rooted out. All our voters have to be made aware of this inexcusable blunder with the water supply.

Dr Stockmann All right; if you think it's in the general interest, go ahead; but not before I've spoken to my brother.

Hovstad In the meantime I shall write an editorial. And if the mayor is not prepared to take any action . . .

Dr Stockmann That's unthinkable!

Hovstad Still, let's think it. Then what . . .?

Dr Stockmann Well, then I promise you . . . listen . . . then you can publish my report . . . unexpurgated.

Hovstad Can I? You give me your word?

Dr Stockmann (*handing him the manuscript*) Here it is; take it with you; can't do any harm for you to read it; you can give it back to me later.

Hovstad Good, right, I'll do that. Goodbye then, Doctor.

Dr Stockmann Goodbye, goodbye. You'll see, it will be a very smooth process, Mr Hovstad . . . very smooth!

Hovstad Hmm . . . we shall see.

He bows and exits through the hall. Dr Stockmann goes over and looks into the dining-room.

Dr Stockmann Katrine . . .! Ah, Petra, you're back!

Petra (*entering*) Yes, I've just come in from school.

Mrs Stockmann (*entering*) Has he not arrived?

Dr Stockmann Peter? No. But I've had quite a talk with Hovstad. He's very impressed with my discovery. And, you see, it does have much wider implications than I first thought. He's put his newspaper at my disposal, if necessary.

Mrs Stockmann Do you think it will be necessary?

Dr Stockmann No, not at all. But it does give you a feeling of pride to have the independent liberal press on your side. Yes, and also . . . I've had a visit from the Chairman of the Property-owners' Association.

Mrs Stockmann Oh? What did he want?

Dr Stockmann To offer his support as well. They all want to support me if things get difficult, Katrine . . . do you realize what it is I have behind me?

Mrs Stockmann Behind you? No; what is it you have behind you?

Dr Stockmann The solid majority.

Mrs Stockmann I see. And is that a good thing, Tomas?

Dr Stockmann It certainly is a good thing! (*He paces up and down, rubbing his hands.*) God, yes, to stand shoulder to shoulder with your fellow-citizens, it's a wonderful feeling!

Petra And to be able to achieve so much, father, good things, useful things!

Dr Stockmann Yes, and for your own home town, as well!

Mrs Stockmann There's the bell.

Dr Stockmann Must be him.

There's a knock at the door.

Come in!

The mayor comes in from the hall.

Mayor Good morning.

Dr Stockmann Nice to see you, Peter!

Mrs Stockmann Good morning. How are you?

Mayor So-so, thank you. (*to the doctor*) Yesterday, after office hours, I received a report from you dealing with the condition of the water at the Baths.

Dr Stockmann Yes. Did you read it?

Mayor I did.

Dr Stockmann And what's your reaction?

Mayor (*with a sidelong glance*) Erm . . .

Mrs Stockmann Come along, Petra.

She and Petra go into the room, stage left.

Mayor (*after a pause*) Was it necessary to carry out all these investigations behind my back?

Dr Stockmann Well, until I was absolutely certain, I . . .

Mayor And now you are?

Dr Stockmann You must know that.

Mayor Do you intend to submit this document to the Board of the Baths, as some kind of official statement?

Dr Stockmann Of course I do. Something has to be done; right away.

Mayor As usual, you've expressed yourself very forcibly in your report. Among other things, you say that what we're offering our visitors to the Baths is irreversible poisoning.

Dr Stockmann Well, Peter, how else would you describe it? Think about it . . . water that's poisonous, whether taken internally or externally! And it's for poor, sick people, who are turning to us in good faith and paying us a fortune to restore their health!

Mayor And your conclusion is that we have to build a

sewer to drain off this alleged filth from the valley, and that the water system will have to be relaid.

Dr Stockmann Yes, can you think of any other alternative? I can't.

Mayor This morning I paid a visit to the municipal engineer. And I put forward these proposals . . . half-jokingly . . . for possible consideration sometime in the future.

Dr Stockmann Sometime in the future!

Mayor Needless to say, he smiled at my hypothetical extravagance. Have you taken the trouble to consider how much these alterations you've suggested might cost? According to the estimates I've received, the expense would probably run to several hundred thousand kroner.

Dr Stockmann As much as that?

Mayor Yes. And that's not the worst of it. The work would take at least two years.

Dr Stockmann Two years, did you say? Two full years?

Mayor At least. And what do we do with the Baths in the meantime? Close them? Yes, we'd be forced to. Or perhaps you think people would come here once the rumour got around that the water carries a health risk?

Dr Stockmann Yes, but, Peter, it does.

Mayor And you choose this moment . . . the precise moment the Baths are starting to succeed. A couple of other towns in the area also have the potential to turn themselves into spas. You think they won't immediately go into action to attract streams of tourists? Of course they will, it's inevitable. So that's the position: we would probably have to close down this whole expensive enterprise; and you would have ruined your home town.

39

Dr Stockmann Ruined it . . . me . . .!

Mayor Those Baths were the only chance this town had of any sort of a worthwhile future. I'm sure you understand that as well as I do.

Dr Stockmann Then what do you think we should do?

Mayor Your report has failed to convince me that the condition of the water at the Baths is as critical as you claim it is.

Dr Stockmann It's more likely to be worse! Or at any rate it will be in the summer, when the weather gets warmer.

Mayor As I've said before, I think you have a penchant for gross exaggeration. A competent doctor should know how to take precautions . . . and be able to suppress harmful consequences or correct them if they become unavoidably conspicuous.

Dr Stockmann So . . .? What are you saying . . .?

Mayor The water being supplied to the Baths is now an established fact and obviously has to be accepted as such. But no doubt, in the fullness of time, the Board will not be unwilling to take into consideration the extent to which it might absorb reasonable financial sacrifices and carry out certain improvements.

Dr Stockmann You think I'd ever agree to such a swindle?

Mayor A swindle?

Dr Stockmann Yes, that's what it would be, a swindle . . . a fraud, a lie, a genuine crime against the public, against the entire community.

Mayor As I said before, I'm not convinced there's any actual immediate danger.

Dr Stockmann Oh, yes, you are! How could you not be?

My paper is incontrovertibly true and accurate, I know that! And so do you, Peter, you know it as well as I do; you just don't want to admit it. You're the one who insisted on siting the Baths and the water supply where they are now. And it's that . . . it's that damned blunder you don't want to acknowledge. Ha . . . do you think I can't see straight through you?

Mayor Suppose you're right? Perhaps I do keep a some-what anxious watch over my reputation, but it's for the benefit of the town. Without moral authority, I can't gov-ern or point things in the direction I consider most con-ducive to the general good. For that reason – and for several others – it's essential to me that your report is not delivered to the Board of Directors. For everybody's sake, it has to be suppressed. Later on, I'll bring the subject up for discussion and we'll do what we can, discreetly; but nothing . . . not a single word about this disastrous busi-ness must be made public.

Dr Stockmann My dear Peter, there's nothing can be done to stop it now.

Mayor It has to be stopped and it will be.

Dr Stockmann I'm telling you, it's not going to work; too many people know about it already.

Mayor Know about it! Who? Not those people from *The People's Messenger*, surely you . . .?

Dr Stockmann Yes, them as well. The independent liberal press will make sure you all do your duty.

Mayor (*after a short pause*) You're an extremely reckless man, Tomas. Have you not considered what consequences this might have for you personally?

Dr Stockmann Consequences? Consequences for me?

Mayor Yes, you and your family.

Dr Stockmann What the hell do you mean?

Mayor You're my brother, I think I've done my duty by you all my life, I've always tried to be helpful.

Dr Stockmann Yes, you have; and I'm grateful to you.

Mayor No need to be. To a certain extent I've done what I had to . . . for selfish reasons. It was always in the hope that if I could help to improve your financial situation, I could somehow get you to show some restraint.

Dr Stockmann What? So it was just for selfish reasons . . .!

Mayor To some extent, I said. It's an embarrassing thing for a civil servant when his nearest relatives make a habit of compromising themselves.

Dr Stockmann Is that what you think I do?

Mayor Yes, I'm afraid you do it without even realizing. You have an unruly, pugnacious, rebellious mind. You have an unfortunate urge to rush into print on any given subject, appropriate or inappropriate. The minute you get some notion . . . you immediately write an article or a whole pamphlet about it.

Dr Stockmann But isn't it a citizen's duty, whenever he has a new idea, to share it with the general public?

Mayor The general public doesn't want new ideas. The general public is happiest with the good, old, familiar ideas it's used to.

Dr Stockmann Well, that's what I call plain speaking!

Mayor Yes, for once I have to speak plainly to you. Up till now, I've been trying to avoid it, I know how touchy you are; but now I must tell you the truth, Tomas. You've no idea how much damage you do to yourself by being so rash. You complain about the authorities, even about the government, yes, you do . . . you're always on the offensive, insisting you've been insulted or persecuted. What else do you expect . . . if you're going to be such a troublemaker.

Dr Stockmann So . . . now I'm a troublemaker?

Mayor Yes, Tomas, you're a very difficult man to work with. I have first-hand experience of that. You don't have the slightest consideration; you seem to have completely forgotten it's me you have to thank for being appointed Medical Officer at the Baths . . .

Dr Stockmann I was entitled to that! More than anyone else! I was the first to see the town could become a flourishing spa; and at the time, I was the only one who saw it. I was out on my own, fighting for the idea all those years; and writing article after article . . .

Mayor No one's denying it. But in those days the time wasn't right; which you weren't in a position to judge, stuck up there in your out-of-the-way corner. As soon as the right moment arrived I . . . and the others . . . took the matter in hand.

Dr Stockmann And proceeded to make a complete mess of my magnificent plan. Oh, yes, a really good illustration of how intelligent you all are!

Mayor In my opinion, it's more of an illustration of your constant urge to find a target for your pugnacity. You want to attack your superiors; . . . you're addicted to it. You can't stand anyone who has authority over you; you don't trust any kind of senior official; you regard him as a personal enemy . . . and immediately, as far as you're concerned, any method of attack is legitimate. But now I've explained to you what's at stake for the whole town . . . and consequently for me as well. And I'm telling you,

Tomas, I'm intending to put a demand to you now, which will not be negotiable.

Dr Stockmann What sort of a demand?

Mayor As you've been garrulous enough to discuss this sensitive issue with outsiders, even though it should have remained an official secret, it's obviously going to be impossible to hush the matter up. All sorts of rumours will spread all over the place and the ill-disposed among us will feed the rumours and embroider them. It's therefore going to be necessary for you to confront these rumours and publicly deny them.

Dr Stockmann Me! How can I? I don't understand what you're saying.

Mayor What we're expecting is for you to undertake some further investigations which will prove that things are not nearly as dangerous or as critical as you imagined at first glance.

Dr Stockmann Ah . . . so that's what you're expecting!

Mayor We're also expecting you to express publicly your genuine confidence in the Board and its ability to be thorough and conscientious and take the necessary steps to root out any possible irregularities.

Dr Stockmann But you'll never be able to do that if you just try to be cunning and cobble things together. I'm telling you, Peter: this is my deepest and most sincere opinion . . .!

Mayor As an employee, you have no right to hold an independent opinion.

Dr Stockmann (*with a start*) No right . . .?

Mayor I'm saying, as an employee. As a private individual . . . good heavens, that's something quite different. But as a minor official of the Baths, you have no right to express any kind of an opinion which might bring you into conflict with your superiors.

Dr Stockmann This is too much! As a doctor, as a scientist, I have no right to . . .!

Mayor The issue we're discussing here is not a purely scientific matter; it's a combination of things; there are technical and economic considerations.

Dr Stockmann What the hell's it matter, what label you stick on it? I want to be free to express myself on any issue whatsoever, anything in the world!

Mayor Fine. But not about the Baths . . . We forbid you to do that.

Dr Stockmann (*shouting*) You forbid me . . .! You! You people . . .!

Mayor I forbid you to do that . . . I do, as your most senior superior; and when I forbid you to do something, you have no choice but to obey.

Dr Stockmann (*restraining himself*) Peter . . . if you weren't my brother . . . I mean it . . .

Petra (*throwing open the door*) Father, you mustn't put up with this!

Mrs Stockmann (*following her*) Petra, Petra!

Mayor Ah, listening in, are we?

Mrs Stockmann You were talking so loud, we couldn't help but . . .

Petra Yes, I was listening.

Mayor Well, I don't suppose it matters.

Dr Stockmann (*moving closer to him*) You were talking

45

to me about forbidding and obeying . . .?

Mayor You forced me to take that tone.

Dr Stockmann And I'm supposed to make a public statement accusing myself of lying?

Mayor We consider it an unavoidable necessity that you publish a statement along the lines I've laid down.

Dr Stockmann And what if I don't . . . obey?

Mayor Then we shall put out a statement ourselves to reassure the public.

Dr Stockmann All right; but then I shall write attacking you. I'm sticking to my guns; I shall prove that I'm right and you're wrong. And then what will you do?

Mayor I shall not be able to prevent your dismissal.

Dr Stockmann What . . .!

Petra Father . . . dismissal!

Mrs Stockmann Dismissal!

Mayor Your dismissal from the post of Medical Officer at the Baths. I'd be forced to call for your immediate resignation and remove you from any kind of further contact with the Baths.

Dr Stockmann And you'd take that risk!

Mayor You're the one who's playing a risky game.

Petra Uncle, this is outrageous behaviour towards a man like my father.

Mrs Stockmann Petra, will you just keep quiet!

Mayor (*looking at Petra*) So, you've already started opinion-mongering. Stands to reason. (*to Mrs Stockmann*) Katrine, you're probably the most sensible

46

person in the house. Use whatever influence you may have over your husband; make him understand how this is likely to affect his family and . . .

Dr Stockmann My family is my concern and nobody else's!

Mayor . . . his family, as I was saying, and the town he lives in.

Dr Stockmann I'm the one who wants what's genuinely best for the town! I want to unmask the failings which are going to have to be revealed sooner or later. Oh, there'll be ample proof of how much I love my home town.

Mayor When you're about to cut off the town's principal source of income out of blind spite?

Dr Stockmann The source is poisoned, man! Are you insane? We're making our living out of peddling filth and corruption! The whole of our flourishing community life is fertilized by a lie!

Mayor It's your imagination . . . or something worse. A man who would spread such damaging insinuations about his own native town must be an enemy of society.

Dr Stockmann (*going for him*) You dare to . . .!

Mrs Stockmann (*throwing herself between them*) Tomas!

Petra (*hanging on to her father's arm*) Stay calm, father!

Mayor I don't intend to expose myself to violence. You've been warned. Think about what you owe yourself and your family. Goodbye. (*He exits.*)

Dr Stockmann (*pacing up and down*) And I'm supposed to put up with being treated like this! In my own house, Katrine! What do you think of that!

Mrs Stockmann Well, it's ridiculous, it's a disgrace, Tomas, no doubt about it . . .

47

Petra If I ever get hold of uncle . . .!

Dr Stockmann It's my own fault; I should have dug my heels in a long time ago . . . shown my teeth . . . and bitten them! And he called me an enemy of society! Me! To say a thing like that about me, by God, I'm not going to stand for it!

Mrs Stockmann But, Tomas darling, it's your brother who has all the power . . .

Dr Stockmann Yes, but I'm the one who's right!

Mrs Stockmann Oh, well, right, right; what's the use of being right, if you have no power?

Petra No, mother . . . how can you say a thing like that?

Dr Stockmann So, in a free society, it's no use having right on your side? You're very odd, Katrine. And besides . . . don't I have the independent liberal press on my side . . . and the solid majority behind me? That's quite enough power, I'd say!

Mrs Stockmann My God, Tomas, you're not thinking of . . .?

Dr Stockmann Not thinking of what?

Mrs Stockmann . . . of setting yourself up against your brother, I was going to say.

Dr Stockmann What the hell else do you want me to do, when I'm told I can't stand up for what's right and true?

Petra Yes, that's exactly my question.

Mrs Stockmann But that's not going to get you anywhere; they don't have to do a thing they don't want to.

Dr Stockmann Ha, Katrine, just give it time, you'll see, I'll win my war.

Mrs Stockmann All you'll win is your dismissal . . . you wait and see.

Dr Stockmann Well, in any case, I will have done my duty by the public . . . by society. The man they call an enemy of society!

Mrs Stockmann But what about your family, Tomas? What about us here at home? Do you think you'll have done your duty by your dependants?

Petra Oh, you mustn't always think of us first, mother.

Mrs Stockmann Well, it's easy for you to talk; if necessary, you can stand on your own two feet . . . But don't forget the boys, Tomas; and have a little consideration for yourself as well, and for me . . .

Dr Stockmann I think you've taken leave of your senses, Katrine! If I prostrate myself in front of Peter and his damned cronies like a miserable coward . . . will I ever in my life have a single moment's happiness?

Mrs Stockmann That I don't know; but God spare us from the happiness that's in store for us all if you go on defying them. You'll be back where you were, no job, no regular income. I'd have thought we'd had enough of that in the old days; don't forget that, Tomas; think what's at stake.

Dr Stockmann (*writhing in inner turmoil and clenching his fists*) And these slaves of the bureaucracy can impose something like this on a free, honest man! Isn't that appalling, Katrine?

Mrs Stockmann Yes, you've been shamefully treated, there's no doubt about it. But, God knows, there's so much injustice in this world that has to be endured . . . Here come the boys, Tomas! Look at them! What's to become of them? Oh, no, no, surely you haven't the heart to . . .

Meanwhile, Ejlif and Morten have entered, carrying their schoolbooks.

Dr Stockmann Boys . . .! (*He stands up, suddenly firm and decisive.*) No, even if the whole world collapses, I refuse to bend my neck to their yoke. (*He moves towards his study.*)

Mrs Stockmann (*following him*) Tomas . . . what are you going to do?

Dr Stockmann (*in the doorway*) I'm going to earn the right to look my boys in the eye on the day they grow to be free men. (*He exits.*)

Mrs Stockmann (*bursting into tears*) Oh, God, help us all!

Petra Father's a hero! He won't give in.

The boys, bewildered, begin to ask what's going on; Petra signals to them to be quiet.

Act Three

The editorial office of The People's Messenger. *The entrance is upstage left; on the same wall, stage right, is another door with glass panes through which the printing-works is visible. There's a door in the stage-right wall. Centre stage is a large table covered with documents, newspapers and books. Downstage left is a window in front of which is a writing-desk with a high stool. A couple of armchairs stand near the table, various other chairs along the walls. The room is gloomy and sinister, the furniture old and the armchairs filthy and ripped. A couple of compositors can be seen at work in the printing-works; further down, a hand press is being operated.*

Hovstad sits at the desk writing. After a while, Billing enters stage right with the doctor's manuscript in his hand.

Billing Well, I must say . . .!

Hovstad (*writing*) Have you read it all?

Billing (*putting the manuscript on the desk*) I certainly have.

Hovstad Pretty hard-hitting, the doctor, don't you think?

Billing Hard-hitting? I'll say, he's bloody devastating. Every word falls with the weight of a . . . well, I'd say a sledgehammer blow.

Hovstad Yes, but it'll take more than one blow to demolish that lot.

Billing You're right; but we'll just go on swinging the

51

hammer . . . blow after blow, until the whole of official-dom collapses. As I sat in there reading, it was as if I could make out the distant shape of the revolution.

Hovstad (*turning*) Ssh; don't let Aslaksen hear you saying that.

Billing (*lowering his voice*) Aslaksen's chicken-hearted, he's yellow; he doesn't have a man's bone in him. But this time you'll surely just impose your will. Won't you? You will publish the doctor's article?

Hovstad Well, if the mayor refuses to give way, we'll . . .

Billing That'd be a damn nuisance.

Hovstad Well, fortunately we can do ourselves a bit of good, whichever way it goes. If the mayor doesn't go along with the doctor's proposition, he'll have all the tradesmen down on him . . . the Property-owners' Association and the rest of them. And if he does go along with it, he'll get himself in trouble with a whole gang of big shareholders at the Baths, who up to now have been his strongest supporters . . .

Billing Yes, of course; they're bound to have to shell out a huge pile of money . . .

Hovstad You said it. And, see, either way, the circle is broken, and then we can use the paper day in and day out to impress on the public that the mayor is completely incompetent and that all the positions of responsibility in the town, the entire council should be put in the hands of the liberals.

Billing Absolutely bloody right! I can see it now . . . I can see it; it's as if we're standing on the threshold of the revolution!

There's a knock at the door.

Hovstad Ssh! (*shouting*) Come in!

Dr Stockmann enters through the upstage left door. Hovstad moves towards him.

Ah, it's the doctor. Well?

Dr Stockmann Start the presses, Mr Hovstad!

Hovstad So it's come to that?

Billing Hurrah!

Dr Stockmann Start the presses, I say. Yes, of course it's come to that. And now they'll get what they're asking for. There's going to be a war in this town, Mr Billing!

Billing A night of the long knives, I hope! A few throats cut, eh, Doctor!

Dr Stockmann My report is only the beginning. My head is already buzzing with ideas for four or five more articles. Where's Aslaksen?

Billing (*shouting into the printing-works*) Aslaksen, come here a minute!

Hovstad Four or five more articles, you say? On the same subject?

Dr Stockmann No . . . far from it, my dear fellow. No, they'll be about quite other matters. But all stemming from the water supply and the sewage system. One thing leads to another, you see. It's like when you start tearing down an old building . . . exactly the same.

Billing Bloody right; you never seem to be finished until the whole eyesore's been torn down.

Aslaksen enters from the printing-works.

Aslaksen Torn down! You're not thinking of tearing down the Baths, are you, Doctor?

Hovstad On the contrary; don't worry.

Dr Stockmann No, we're talking about something completely different. So, what do you think of my report, Mr Hovstad?

Hovstad I think it's a genuine masterpiece . . .

Dr Stockmann It is, isn't it . . .? Well, I'm so pleased; I'm so pleased.

Hovstad It's so clear and so straightforward; you don't have to be any sort of an expert to be able to work out the implications. I imagine you'll have every single intelligent man on your side.

Aslaksen And every reasonable man as well?

Billing Reasonable and unreasonable . . . that covers almost the whole town.

Aslaksen Well then, I think we might venture to publish it.

Dr Stockmann Yes, I should think so!

Hovstad It'll go in tomorrow morning.

Dr Stockmann Damn it, yes, we mustn't waste a single day. Listen, Mr Aslaksen, I wanted to ask you something: you must look after the manuscript yourself.

Aslaksen I will.

Dr Stockmann Take care of it as if it were made of gold. No misprints; every word is essential. And I'll look in a bit later; do a spot of proof-reading . . . Yes, I can't tell you how much I long to see it in print . . . blazing out . . .

Billing Blazing out . . . that's right, like lightning!

Dr Stockmann . . . open to the judgement of every thinking man. Oh, you'd never believe what I've been subjected to today. I've had all sorts of threats; they've tried to take away my most fundamental human rights . . .

Billing Your human rights? What!

Dr Stockmann . . . they've tried to degrade me, take away my self-respect, they've pressured me to put personal advantage above my deepest and most sacred convictions . . .

Billing Bloody outrageous!

Hovstad Well, yes, what else would you expect from those people?

Dr Stockmann But with me, they've hit a brick wall; they're going to get it in black and white. I'm going to drop anchor in *The People's Messenger* every single day and bombard them with one exploding article after another . . .

Aslaksen Yes, but just a minute . . .

Billing Hurrah; it's war, it's war!

Dr Stockmann . . . I'm going to batter them to the ground, I'm going to crush them, I'm going to blast through their defences in front of every right-thinking person. That's what I'm going to do!

Aslaksen As long as you're moderate about it, Doctor; attack with moderation . . .

Billing No, no, no, no! Don't hold back with the dynamite!

Dr Stockmann (*continuing imperturbably*) Because, you see, this isn't just about the water supply and the sewage system. It's the whole of society which needs cleaning out and disinfecting . . .

Billing Yes, that's the key word!

Dr Stockmann It's time to sweep away all those shoddy old second-raters, you see. From every corner! Such endless vistas have opened up for me today. Nothing's quite clear to me yet; but it will be. We must go out and look for fresh, young standard-bearers, my friends; we need new commanders for all the advance posts.

Billing Hear, hear!

Dr Stockmann All we need is to stick together and everything will go very smoothly, very smoothly! A whole revolution will glide off the stocks like a liner. Don't you think?

Hovstad As far as I'm concerned, this is a chance for us all to transfer control of the council now, to where it really belongs.

Aslaksen And as long as we forge ahead with moderation, I can't think we'll be in any danger.

Dr Stockmann What the hell difference does it make, whether we're in any danger? What I'm doing, I'm doing in the name of truth and for the sake of my own conscience.

Hovstad You're a man who deserves support, Doctor.

Aslaksen Yes, it's undeniable, the doctor's a true friend to this town; a genuine friend of society.

Billing Doctor Stockmann's a bloody friend of the people, Aslaksen!

Aslaksen I'm sure the Property-owners' Association will soon acknowledge him as such.

Dr Stockmann (*moved, pressing their hands*) Thank you, thank you, my dear and faithful friends; . . . it's so satisfying to hear you say these things . . . my brother called me something quite different. Well, I'll pay him back for that, with interest! Now I have to go and see some poor wretched patient . . . As I said, I'll be back. You take good care of that manuscript, Mr Aslaksen; . . . and don't cut any of the exclamation marks, whatever you do! Better if you add a few! Good, all right; goodbye for now; goodbye, goodbye!

General salutations as they accompany him to the door and he exits.

Hovstad He could be invaluable to us.

Aslaksen Yes, as long as he confines himself to dealing with the Baths. Whereas if he goes any further, it wouldn't be advisable to support him.

Hovstad Hm, I suppose it depends what . . .

Billing You're always so damned timid, Aslaksen.

Aslaksen Timid? Yes, as far as the local powers-that-be are concerned, I am timid, Mr Billing; it's something I've learned in the university of life, let me tell you. But when it comes to the broader political scene, you can set me up against the government itself and then see how timid I am.

Billing No, I know you aren't, no; that's exactly what's so paradoxical about you.

Aslaksen The thing is, I'm a man of conscience. If you attack the government, it does no harm to society whatsoever; because, you see, they don't take a blind bit of notice; . . . they just carry on regardless. Whereas the *local* authorities can be brought down, and then you get a danger of inexperience at the helm, which could cause irreparable damage to property-owners and everybody else.

Hovstad What about self-government as a means of educating the individual citizen . . . don't you believe in that?

Aslaksen If a man has something in his hands that's worth hanging on to, there's a limit to what he can believe in, Mr Hovstad.

Hovstad Then I hope I never have anything like that in my hands!

Billing Hear, hear!

Aslaksen (*smiling*) Hm. (*He points at the desk.*) Before you sat at that editor's desk, it was occupied by District Councillor Stensgård.

Billing (*spitting*) Hah! That time-server.

Hovstad I'm no turncoat . . . and I never will be.

Aslaksen A politician should never rule out any possibility, Mr Hovstad. And you might be wise to reef in a sail or two, Mr Billing, I'd say; as you're standing for Secretary to the Magistrate.

Billing I . . .!

Hovstad Is that right, Billing?

Billing Well . . . you can be damn sure it's only to annoy the hierarchy.

Aslaksen Well, it's none of my business. But when I'm accused of being cowardly or holding paradoxical opinions, there's one thing I like to stress: Aslaksen the printer's political past is an open book to one and all. I've never changed my mind, you see, except that I've become a little more moderate. My heart still belongs to the people; but I can't deny that my head inclines towards the powers-that-be . . . at any rate, the local ones. (*He goes into the printing-works.*)

Billing Can't we get rid of him, Hovstad?

Hovstad Do you know anyone else who's prepared to

give us credit for newsprint and printing costs?

Billing It's a damn nuisance we have no working capital.

Hovstad (*sitting at his desk*) Yes, if we did have . . .

Billing What about going to Doctor Stockmann?

Hovstad (*riffling through some papers*) Ha, what use would that be? He's not worth anything.

Billing No; but he has a good man behind him, old Morten Kiil . . . otherwise known as the Badger.

Hovstad (*writing*) Are you sure he's worth anything?

Billing Course he bloody is! And a good deal of it must be headed for Stockmann's family. He has to be thinking of providing . . . at least for the children.

Hovstad (*half-turning*) Are you banking on that?

Billing Banking? Course not, I'm not banking on anything.

Hovstad Quite right. And that job in the Magistrate's office, I shouldn't bank on that either; because I'm telling you . . . you're not going to get it.

Billing You think I'm not well aware of that? That's precisely what's important to me, not to get it. A setback like that sparks off your fighting spirit; . . . it's like a dose of fresh bile, and that's what you need in an out-of-the-way dump like this, where it's so rare for something really infuriating to happen.

Hovstad (*writing*) Yes, yes.

Billing Well . . . they'll soon be hearing from me! . . . I'm going in to write that appeal to the Property-owners' Association.

He exits through the stage-right door. Hovstad sits at his desk, chewing the end of his pen.

Hovstad (*slowly*) Mm . . . yes, right.

There's a knock at the door.

Come in!

Petra comes in through the entrance, upstage left.
Hovstad stands up.

Oh, it's you. You've come down here?

Petra Yes, I'm sorry . . .

Hovstad (*pulling up an armchair*) Won't you sit down?

Petra No, thanks; I can't stay.

Hovstad Have you brought something from your father, perhaps?

Petra No, I've brought something from me. (*She takes a book out of the pocket of her cloak.*) It's that English story.

Hovstad Why are you bringing it back?

Petra Because I don't want to translate it.

Hovstad But you promised me . . .

Petra I hadn't read it then. And you haven't read it either, have you?

Hovstad No; you know I don't understand English; but . . .

Petra No; so I wanted to tell you, you'll have to look for something else. (*She puts the book down on the table.*) You can't print this in *The Messenger*.

Hovstad Why not?

Petra Because it completely contradicts all your own opinions.

Hovstad Oh, so that's why . . .

Petra I don't think you understand me. It's about how some supernatural force takes care of all the so-called good people in the world and makes sure everything works out well for them in the end . . . and how all the so-called wicked people are punished.

Hovstad Very good. That's exactly what people want.

Petra Do you want to be responsible for giving people this sort of stuff? When you don't believe a word of it. You know very well, this has nothing to do with reality.

Hovstad You're absolutely right; but an editor can't always do what he most wants to. Often, in less import-ant matters, he has to bow to public opinion. Politics, that's still the priority in people's lives . . . for a newspa-per, at least; and if I want people to join me in supporting freedom and progress, I mustn't frighten them off. If they find some moral tale buried away in the back pages, they find it much easier to accept what we print on the front page; . . . it makes them feel more secure.

Petra Shame on you; you're not so deceitful you have to lay traps for your readers; you're not a spider.

Hovstad (*smiling*) Thanks, for thinking so well of me. No, as a matter of fact, this was Billing's idea, not mine.

Petra Billing!

Hovstad Yes, at least that's what he's been saying these last few days. It's Billing who's so keen to run this story; I don't even know the book.

Petra But Billing is a man of progressive views, how can he . . .?

Hovstad Oh, there are several sides to Billing. I hear he's now applying for the post of Secretary to the Magistrate.

Petra I don't think so, Hovstad. How could he bring himself to do a thing like that?

Hovstad You'll have to ask him.

Petra I'd never have believed this of Billing.

Hovstad (*looking at her more closely*) No? Is it really so unexpected?

Petra Yes. Or perhaps not, after all. Oh, I really don't know . . .

Hovstad We journalists aren't good for much, Miss Petra.

Petra Do you really mean that?

Hovstad I sometimes think so.

Petra Yes, when it's bickering business as usual, I can understand it. But now you've taken up this great cause . . .

Hovstad This thing of your father's, you mean?

Petra Exactly. Surely now you must feel like a man who's good for most things.

Hovstad Yes, today I do feel something of the sort.

Petra Yes, you must, mustn't you? Oh, what you've chosen is such a wonderful vocation. To clear a path for unrecognized truths and for brave new visions . . . ; yes, just to take a stand and speak up fearlessly for a wronged man . . .

Hovstad Especially when the wronged man is . . . hm . . . I don't quite know how to put this . . .

Petra When he's so upright and fundamentally honest, you mean?

Hovstad (*quieter*) I meant, especially when he's your father.

Petra (*suddenly realizing*) So that's it?

Hovstad Yes, Petra . . . Miss Petra.

Petra Was *that* the most important thing to you? Not the cause itself? Not the truth; not father's great, generous heart?

Hovstad Yes . . . well, obviously, that as well.

Petra No, thanks; you've given yourself away now, Hovstad; and from now on I'll never believe a word you say.

Hovstad How can you be so offended that it's principally for your sake . . .?

Petra The reason I'm angry with you is that you haven't been honest with father. You've given him the impression that truth and the good of society are what's uppermost in your mind. You've cheated father and me; you're not the man you pretended to be. And I'll never forgive you for that . . . never!

Hovstad You shouldn't speak to me so harshly, Miss Petra; especially not now.

Petra What do you mean, why not now?

Hovstad Because your father can't do without my help.

Petra (*looking down at him*) You as well, is that what you're like? Shame on you!

Hovstad No, no, I'm not; it just slipped out inadvertently; you mustn't think that.

Petra I know what to think. Goodbye.

Aslaksen hurries in from the printing-works, his manner secretive.

Aslaksen Damn it, Mr Hovstad . . . (*He sees Petra.*) Oh, my God . . .

63

Petra I'm leaving the book here; you'll have to give it to someone else.

She moves towards the entrance. Hovstad follows her.

Hovstad But, Miss . . .

Petra Goodbye. (*She exits.*)

Aslaksen Listen, Mr Hovstad!

Hovstad Well, yes; what is it now?

Aslaksen The mayor's out there in the printing-works.

Hovstad Did you say the mayor?

Aslaksen Yes, he wants to talk to you; he came in the back way . . . as you can imagine, he doesn't want to be seen.

Hovstad What can this be about? No, wait, I'll do it . . . (*He crosses to the door to the printing-works, greets the mayor and invites him in.*) Keep a lookout, Aslaksen, so no one . . .

Aslaksen Understood . . . (*He exits to the printing-works.*)

Mayor I don't suppose you expected to see me here, Mr Hovstad.

Hovstad No, I certainly didn't.

Mayor (*looking around*) You've made yourself very comfortable; really nice.

Hovstad Oh . . .

Mayor And I turn up without an appointment, taking up your valuable time.

Hovstad Not at all, I'm at your service, Mr Mayor. May I take your . . .? (*He puts the mayor's cap and stick on a chair.*) Won't you sit down, sir?

Mayor Thank you.

He sits by the table; Hovstad sits opposite.

I've had a . . . something extremely annoying has happened today, Mr Hovstad.

Hovstad Really? Well; I imagine, with all your commitments as mayor, there . . .

Mayor The origin of this business today is the Medical Officer at the Baths.

Hovstad Oh, yes; you mean the doctor?

Mayor He's written a kind of report to the Board at the Baths concerning a number of alleged defects found in the Baths.

Hovstad He hasn't, has he?

Mayor Yes, didn't he tell you . . .? I thought he said he . . .

Hovstad Oh yes, that's right, he did mention something . . .

Aslaksen (*from the printing-works*) I need that manuscript . . .

Hovstad (*annoyed*) Erm; there it is on the desk.

Aslaksen (*finding it*) Good.

Mayor But that's exactly what . . .

Aslaksen Yes, that's the doctor's article, Mr Mayor.

Hovstad Oh, so *that's* what you were talking about?

Mayor Precisely. What do you think of it?

Hovstad I'm no expert, I just skimmed through it.

Mayor But you're allowing it to be published?

Hovstad It's a signed piece, I can't very well . . .

Aslaksen I have no influence on the paper, Mr Mayor . .

Mayor Of course not.

Aslaksen I just print what they put in front of me.

Mayor Absolutely.

Aslaksen Well, I'd better be . . . (*He starts moving towards the printing-works.*)

Mayor No, just a minute, Mr Aslaksen. If you don't mind, Mr Hovstad . . .

Hovstad Please . . .

Mayor You're a thoughtful and reflective man, Mr Aslaksen.

Aslaksen I'm pleased you think so, Mr Mayor.

Mayor And a man with a wide circle of influence.

Aslaksen Mostly among small tradespeople, I'd say.

Mayor Here, like everywhere else . . . there are more small taxpayers than any other sort.

Aslaksen Very true.

Mayor And I've no doubt you have a sense of their general mood. Am I right?

Aslaksen Yes, I daresay you are, Mr Mayor.

Mayor Well . . . since such an admirable spirit of self-sacrifice prevails among the town's less privileged citizens, I . . .

Aslaksen What?

Hovstad Self-sacrifice?

Mayor It's a beautiful, public-spirited gesture; a most beautiful gesture. I was about to say, it was something I hadn't expected. But you of course have a far deeper sense of their general mood than I.

Aslaksen Well, yes, Mr Mayor, but . . .

Mayor And it's certainly no small sacrifice the town's going to have to make.

Hovstad The town?

Aslaksen But I don't understand . . . Surely it's the Baths . . .!

Mayor At a provisional estimate, the alterations recommended by the Medical Officer at the Baths will run to several hundred thousand kroner.

Aslaksen It's a lot of money; but . . .

Mayor Of course it will be necessary for us to raise a community loan.

Hovstad (*getting up*) Surely you don't mean the town . . .?

Aslaksen Are you talking about a local tax? From the pockets of our poor tradesmen?

Mayor Well, yes, Mr Aslaksen, where else is the money going to come from?

Aslaksen The shareholders at the Baths, it's their responsibility.

Mayor The shareholders don't see themselves in a position to extend themselves any further than they have already.

Aslaksen Are you quite certain of that, Mr Mayor?

Mayor There's no doubt in my mind. If alterations this extensive are required, then the town will have to pay for them.

Aslaksen But, goddamn it . . . oh, I beg your pardon! . . . this is quite another matter, Mr Hovstad.

Hovstad It certainly is.

Mayor The most disastrous thing is, we're going to have to close the Baths for a couple of years.

Hovstad Close them? Close them altogether!

Aslaksen For two years!

Mayor Yes, that's how long the work will take . . . at least.

Aslaksen No, damn it, we'll never manage that, Mr Mayor! We property-owners, how are we supposed to live in the meantime?

Mayor I'm afraid that's an extremely difficult question to answer, Mr Aslaksen. But what can we do? Do you suppose we'll get a single tourist here, once people start going around saying the water is polluted, the ground we live on is infected, the whole town is . . .

Aslaksen And he could have imagined the whole thing?

Mayor With the best will in the world, I can't persuade myself otherwise.

Aslaksen Well, then, it's quite inexcusable of Doctor Stockmann to . . . I beg your pardon, Mr Mayor, but . . .

Mayor Regrettably, Mr Aslaksen, what you're saying is true. I'm afraid my brother has always been an impetuous man.

Aslaksen And you still want to support him in this, Mr Hovstad?

Hovstad Well, who could have imagined that . . .?

Mayor I've set out a short account of the matter, an inter-

68

pretation from a sensible standpoint; and in addition, I've suggested reasonable ways for any possible problems to be put right, using methods which are financially feasible for the Baths.

Hovstad Do you have the piece on you, Mr Mayor?

Mayor (*fumbling in his pocket*) Yes; I brought it just in case you . . .

Aslaksen (*hurriedly*) Damn it, here he is!

Mayor Who? My brother?

Hovstad Where . . . where?

Aslaksen He's coming through the printing-works.

Mayor Disaster. I don't want to meet him here, but I do have several other things to discuss with you.

Hovstad points to the door, stage right.

Hovstad Wait in there.

Mayor But . . .?

Hovstad There's no one in there but Billing.

Aslaksen Quick, Mr Mayor; he's coming.

Mayor Yes, all right; make sure you get rid of him soon.

He exits through the door, stage right, which Aslaksen opens and closes for him.

Hovstad Find yourself something to do, Aslaksen.

He sits down and starts writing. Aslaksen rummages through a pile of newspapers on a chair, stage right. Dr Stockmann comes in from the printing-works.

Dr Stockmann Here I am again. (*He puts down his hat and stick.*)

Hovstad (*writing*) Already, Doctor? Can you get on with what we were talking about, Aslaksen? Time's very short today.

Dr Stockmann (*to Aslaksen*) So, no proofs to check, I gather.

Aslaksen (*without turning back*) No, surely you weren't expecting them, Doctor?

Dr Stockmann No, no; but you can understand how impatient I am. I shan't be able to relax, until I see it in print.

Hovstad Hm; I'm sure it'll be quite a while. Don't you think, Aslaksen?

Aslaksen Yes, I'm afraid so.

Dr Stockmann All right, all right, my dear friends; I'll come back; if necessary, I'll come back twice. This is so important . . . the whole town's welfare . . . ; my God, it's no time to be loafing about. (*He starts to go, then stops and turns back.*) Oh, listen . . . there is just one other thing I need to talk to you about.

Hovstad I'm sorry; can't we discuss it later . . .?

Dr Stockmann Won't take a minute. It's just that, you see . . . when they read my article in the paper tomorrow and find out I've spent the whole winter quietly working away for the good of the town . . .

Hovstad Yes, but, Doctor . . .

Dr Stockmann I know what you're going to say. You think it was no more than doing my damned job . . . a simple civic duty. Well, of course, I know that as well as you do. But it's the townspeople, you see . . . ; my God, the dear old things, they're so fond of me . . .

Aslaksen Yes, Doctor, the people have always been very fond of you in the past.

Dr Stockmann Yes, this is just what I'm afraid of . . . ; this is exactly what I meant: when they read this . . . especially the less well-off . . . like a manifesto encouraging them to take the town's future into their own hands . . .

Hovstad (*getting up*) Erm, Doctor, I won't conceal from you . . .

Dr Stockmann Aha . . . I thought there was something going on! But I'm not going to allow it. If they're preparing one of those . . .

Hovstad What?

Dr Stockmann You know, one of those things . . . a torch-light parade or a gala dinner or a subscription towards some commemorative gift . . . or whatever it might be, you're to give me your solemn promise you'll put a stop to it. And you too, Mr Aslaksen; you hear me!

Hovstad I'm sorry, Doctor; we may as well tell you the truth sooner rather than later . . .

Mrs Stockmann enters through the upstage-left door, in her hat and cloak.

Mrs Stockmann (*seeing the doctor*) Yes, I thought so!

Hovstad (*moving towards her*) Look, your wife's here.

Dr Stockmann What the hell are you doing here, Katrine?

Mrs Stockmann You know very well what I'm doing here.

Hovstad Won't you sit down? Or would you . . .

Mrs Stockmann Never mind, thanks. And you mustn't take it amiss that I've come to fetch Stockmann; after all,

I am the mother of three children.

Dr Stockmann Yes, yes; we all know that.

Mrs Stockmann Well, it doesn't look as if you're giving much thought to your wife and children today, otherwise why would you go off and drag us all down to ruin?

Dr Stockmann Have you taken leave of your senses, Katrine? Just because he has a wife and children, is a man not allowed to tell the truth . . .? Is he not allowed to be a useful and effective citizen . . .? Is he not allowed to be of service to his home town?

Mrs Stockmann Moderation in all things, Tomas!

Aslaksen That's what I always say. Moderation in all things.

Mrs Stockmann And that's how you've betrayed us, Mr Hovstad, luring my husband away from home and tricking him into all this.

Hovstad I assure you I haven't tricked anyone . . .

Dr Stockmann Tricked! You think I'd let myself be tricked!

Mrs Stockmann Of course you would. I know you're the cleverest man in this town; but you're a very easy man to trick, Tomas. (*to Hovstad*) You just think about this, if you print what he's written, he's going to lose his job at the Baths.

Aslaksen What?

Hovstad Listen, Doctor . . .

Dr Stockmann (*laughing*) Ha ha, just let them try it . . .! No, my dear, they wouldn't dare. You see, I have the solid majority behind me!

Mrs Stockmann Yes, that's exactly what's going to ruin you, to have something that ugly behind you.

Dr Stockmann Nonsense, Katrine; . . . go home and look after the house and let me take care of society. What's there to be afraid about, when I'm so confident and happy? (*He rubs his hands, pacing up and down.*) The truth and the people will be victorious, you can bank on it. Oh, I can see every liberal in the town banding together to form a conquering army . . .! (*He stops by a chair.*) What . . . what the hell is that?

Aslaksen (*looking*) Oops!

Hovstad (*likewise*) Erm . . .

Dr Stockmann It's the topknot of authority. (*He picks up the mayor's official cap gingerly with his fingertips and holds it up in the air.*)

Mrs Stockmann The mayor's cap!

Dr Stockmann And here's his sceptre. What on earth's going on . . .?

Hovstad Well . . .

Dr Stockmann Oh, I see! He's been round to try and talk you out of it. Ha ha, showing his usual good judgement! And when he saw me coming through the printing-works . . . (*He bursts out laughing.*) Did he run for it, Mr Aslaksen?

Aslaksen (*hastily*) God, yes, he ran for it, Doctor.

Dr Stockmann Ran and left his stick and . . . Rubbish; Peter never runs away from anything. Now, what the hell have you done with him? Ah . . . must be in there. Now, watch this, Katrine!

Mrs Stockmann Tomas . . . I'm begging you . . .!

Aslaksen Take care, Doctor!

Dr Stockmann has put the mayor's cap on his head and picked up his stick, then he crosses to the door, opens it and salutes. The mayor enters, red with anger. Billing follows him out.

Mayor What's the meaning of this pandemonium?

Dr Stockmann Behave yourself, my dear Peter. I'm in charge of the town now. (*He parades up and down.*)

Mrs Stockmann (*almost in tears*) Stop it, Tomas, please!

Mayor (*pursuing him*) Give me my cap and stick!

Dr Stockmann (*as before*) Why don't you be chief of police and I'll be mayor . . . as you can see, I'm the town's supreme commander!

Mayor Take off that cap, I said. That is a regulation official cap, I'll have you know!

Dr Stockmann Hah; the people are stirring like a waking lion, you think you can frighten them off with official caps? Yes, we're going to have a revolution in the town tomorrow, it's time you knew. You threatened to dismiss me; well, now I dismiss you . . . I dismiss you from all your posts . . . You think I can't? Well, listen to this; I have the conquering armies of society on my side. Hovstad and Billing are going to thunder in *The People's Messenger*, and Aslaksen is advancing at the head of the Property-owners' Association.

Aslaksen No, I'm not, Doctor.

Dr Stockmann Of course you are . . .

Mayor Aha; so Mr Hovstad is choosing to join the agitators after all, is he?

Hovstad No, Mr Mayor.

Aslaksen No, Mr Hovstad's not mad enough to destroy himself and his newspaper because of something you've imagined.

Dr Stockmann (*looking around*) What does this mean?

Hovstad You've presented your case in a false light, Doctor; that's why I can't support you.

Billing And after what the mayor has been kind enough to explain to me in there, I . . .

Dr Stockmann Lies! Let me deal with this. Just publish my article; I'm man enough to defend it.

Hovstad I won't publish it. I cannot, will not and dare not publish it.

Dr Stockmann You dare not? What kind of talk is this? You're the editor; and it's the editors who control the press I'd have thought, surely!

Aslaksen No, Doctor, it's the readers.

Mayor Fortunately.

Aslaksen It's public opinion, an enlightened readership, property-owners and so on; that's who control the press.

Dr Stockmann (*calmly*) And all these powers are against me?

Aslaksen They are, yes. It would mean the complete collapse of the middle-classes, if your article was published.

Dr Stockmann I see . . .

Mayor My cap and my stick!

Dr Stockmann takes off the cap and lays it on the table with the stick. The mayor picks them up.

Your term of office came to a sudden end.

Dr Stockmann It's not over yet. (*to Hovstad*) So it's impossible to put my article in *The Messenger*?

Hovstad Quite impossible; out of consideration for your family.

Mrs Stockmann Oh, please don't concern yourself about our family, Mr Hovstad.

The mayor takes a document out of his pocket.

Mayor When this comes out, it'll be sufficient for the purposes of public information; it's an authentic clarification. If you'll be so kind.

Hovstad (*taking the document*) Right; it'll be printed immediately.

Dr Stockmann And mine won't. You imagine you can silence me and the truth! But this is not going to go as smoothly as you think. Mr Aslaksen, please take my manuscript immediately and print it as a pamphlet . . . at my own expense . . . I'll publish it myself. I shall want four hundred copies; no, five . . . six hundred, I'll be wanting.

Aslaksen Not if you offered me gold, Doctor, I wouldn't dare use my press for something like this. I wouldn't dare insult public opinion. You won't get this printed anywhere in town.

Dr Stockmann Then give it back.

Hovstad (*handing him the manuscript*) Here you are.

Dr Stockmann fetches his hat and stick.

Dr Stockmann All the same it is going to come out. I shall find some big public assembly and read it aloud; all my fellow-citizens are going to hear the voice of truth.

Mayor No organization in the town will give you space to do that.

Aslaksen Not a single one; I'm convinced of it.

Billing Not bloody likely!

Mrs Stockmann This is a complete disgrace! Why have they turned against you, every single one of them?

Dr Stockmann (*angrily*) Well, I'll tell you. It's because in this town all the men are nothing but old women . . . like you; they're all just thinking about their families and not about society as a whole.

Mrs Stockmann (*seizing his arm*) Then I'll show them . . . that for once in a while . . . an old woman can be a man. I'm on your side now, Tomas!

Dr Stockmann Very bravely said, Katrine. And it is going to come out, by everything that's sacred! If I can't rent a space, I'll hire a drummer to go round the town with me and I'll read it aloud on every street corner.

Mayor You can't be so completely insane!

Dr Stockmann Yes, I can.

Aslaksen You won't find a single man in the whole town to go with you.

Billing No, you bloody won't!

Mrs Stockmann Just don't give in, Tomas. I'll ask the boys to go with you.

Dr Stockmann Excellent idea!

Mrs Stockmann Morten will be happy to; and Ejlif'll come too, I'm sure he will.

Dr Stockmann Yes, and Petra, of course! And you, Katrine!

Mrs Stockmann No, not me, no; but I'll stand at the window and watch you; that's what I'll do.

Dr Stockmann takes her in his arms and kisses her.

Dr Stockmann Thank you! So, gentlemen, now you have a fight on your hands! I want to see if mean-spiritedness has the power to gag the patriot, who wants to clean up society!

He and his wife exit, upstage left. The mayor shakes his head thoughtfully.

Mayor Now he's driven her insane as well!

Act Four

*A big old-fashioned room in Captain Horster's house.
Open double doors upstage lead to the front room.
There are three windows in the stage-left wall; in the
middle of the facing wall is a dais, on which is a small
table with two candles, a carafe of water, a glass and a
bell. Further lighting is provided by sconces between the
windows. Downstage left is a table with a candle and a
chair. Downstage right is a door, with a couple of chairs
near by.*

*A large assembly of townspeople of every class. A few
women and some schoolchildren are among the crowd.
More and more people gradually stream in from the back,
filling up the room.*

A Citizen (*bumping into another*) You here this evening
as well, Lamstad?

2nd Citizen Oh, yes, I never miss a public meeting.

3rd Citizen (*standing near by*) Brought your whistle
along, I expect?

2nd Citizen Oh, God, yes. What about you?

3rd Citizen You bet. And skipper Evensen said he was
going to bring along a dirty great horn.

2nd Citizen He's a character, Evensen.

Laughter in the group.

4th Citizen (*joining them*) Listen, tell me, what's supposed to be happening here this evening?

79

2nd Citizen It's Doctor Stockmann, he wants to make a speech attacking the mayor.

4th Citizen But the mayor's his brother.

1st Citizen He doesn't care; Doctor Stockmann's not afraid of anybody.

3rd Citizen But he's wrong; that's what it said in *The Messenger*.

2nd Citizen Yes, he must be wrong this time; they wouldn't let him use the hall at the Property-owners' Association or at the Town Club.

1st Citizen They wouldn't even let him use the Baths.

2nd Citizen Well, you can understand why.

A Man (*in a different group*) Which side are we supposed to support in this thing?

Another (*next to him*) Just watch Aslaksen the printer and do whatever he does.

Billing makes his way through the crowd, a briefcase under his arm.

Billing Mind yourselves, gentlemen! Can you just let me through. I'm reporting on this for *The People's Messenger*. Thanks very much. (*He sits at the table, stage left.*)

A Worker Who's that?

2nd Worker Don't you know him? That's Billing, he works for Aslaksen's newspaper.

Captain Horster leads Mrs Stockmann and Petra in through the downstage-right door. Ejlif and Morten are following.

Horster I thought the family might sit here; then you can easily slip away, if anything happens.

Mrs Stockmann Are you expecting trouble?

Horster You never know . . . ; when there're so many people about . . . Anyway, sit down and make yourself comfortable.

Mrs Stockmann (*sitting down*) It was kind of you to let Stockmann use this place.

Horster Since no one else wanted to . . .

Petra (*who has also sat down*) And it was brave of you too, Horster.

Horster Oh, not as brave as all that, I don't think.

Hovstad and Aslaksen make their way through the crowd, separately, but at the same time. Aslaksen comes over to Horster.

Aslaksen Hasn't the doctor arrived?

Horster He's waiting in there.

There's a commotion by the upstage doors.

Hovstad (*to Billing*) That'll be the mayor. You wait!

Billing Couldn't bloody stay away, after all!

The mayor moves calmly through the crowd, greeting people politely and stops by the wall, stage left. Shortly afterwards, Dr Stockmann enters through the down-stage-right door. He's wearing a black frock-coat and a white tie. There's scattered, uncertain applause, countered by subdued hissing. Silence falls.

Dr Stockmann (*in an undertone*) How are you feeling, Katrine?

Mrs Stockmann I'm fine. (*quieter*) Try not to lose your temper, Tomas.

Dr Stockmann Oh, I know how to control myself. (*He looks at his watch, steps up on to the dais and bows*.) It's a quarter past . . . time to start, I think . . . (*He takes out his manuscript*.)

Aslaksen First, we need to elect a chairman.

Dr Stockmann No, that won't be necessary.

Various Gentlemen (*shouting*) Yes, yes!

Mayor I would have thought we are going to need someone to direct the proceedings.

Dr Stockmann But, Peter, I've called this meeting in order to deliver a lecture!

Mayor It's possible that a lecture given by the Medical Officer at the Baths might give rise to some differences of opinion.

Several Voices (*from the crowd*) A chairman! A director!

Hovstad Public opinion seems to demand a chairman.

Dr Stockmann (*restraining himself*) All right; let public opinion have its way.

Aslaksen Perhaps the mayor might be kind enough to take on the task?

Three Gentlemen (*applauding*) Bravo! Bravo!

Mayor For a number of reasons you'll easily appreciate, I feel obliged to decline. But fortunately we have in our midst a man I feel sure will be acceptable to all. I refer to the Chairman of the Property-owners' Association, Mr Aslaksen.

Many Voices Yes, yes! Long live Aslaksen! Hurrah for Aslaksen!

Dr Stockmann gathers up his manuscript and steps down from the dais.

Aslaksen In the face of such an expression of confidence, I shan't put up any resistance . . .

Applause and cheering. Aslaksen steps up to the dais.

Billing (*writing*) So . . . 'Mr Aslaksen's election was generally acclaimed . . .'

Aslaksen Now I'm standing up here in this position, perhaps I might take the liberty of making a few brief remarks. I'm a quiet, peace-loving sort of chap, who stands for reasonable moderation and . . . and moderation within reason; that much is clear to anyone who knows me.

Many Voices Yes! Hear, hear, Aslaksen!

Aslaksen I've learned from my experience in the university of life that moderation is the most beneficial of all civic virtues . . .

Mayor Hear, hear!

Aslaksen . . . and that reason and moderation are also the qualities which serve society best. I should therefore like to request the respected gentleman who has called this meeting to make every effort to stay within the bounds of moderation.

A Man (*upstage by the doors*) Let's drink to the Temperance Society!

A Voice Shame!

Many Voices Ssh, ssh!

Aslaksen Please, no interruptions, gentlemen! . . . Now, is there anyone who would like to speak?

Mayor Mr Chairman!

Aslaksen The mayor, Mr Stockmann, has the floor.

Mayor Given the fact, which I take to be common knowledge, of my close relationship with the acting Medical Officer at the Baths, I should have much preferred not to have to say anything here this evening. But my own position at the Baths and my concern for the town's most essential interests force me to table a resolution. I make so bold as to assume that not a single one of you present here would consider it desirable for exaggerated accounts of the sanitary conditions at the Baths and in the town to reach external circles.

Many Voices No, no, no! Never! We protest!

Mayor I should therefore like to move that the assembled company does not give the Medical Officer at the Baths permission to read out his lecture on the subject.

Dr Stockmann (*bursting out*) Not give permission . . .! What is this!

Mrs Stockmann (*coughing*) Hm . . . hm!

Dr Stockmann (*restraining himself*) All right; don't give permission.

Mayor In my statement in *The People's Messenger*, I have set forth for the general public all the essential facts, so that every fair-minded citizen can easily form his own opinion. You can see from this that what the Medical Officer at the Baths is proposing – quite apart from constituting a vote of no confidence in the town's most distinguished representatives – basically involves burdening the taxpayers of this town with an unnecessary expenditure of at least a hundred thousand kroner.

Unrest and a certain amount of whistle-blowing.
Aslaksen rings the bell.

Aslaksen Order, gentlemen! I should like to take the liberty of seconding the mayor's motion. I'm in agreement with him that this demonstration of the doctor's has an ulterior motive. He's talking about the Baths; but what he's working towards is a revolution; he wants control to pass into a different set of hands. No one is doubting the doctor's integrity; good Lord, there can be no two opinions on that subject. I'm also sympathetic to the idea of self-government by the people, as long as it doesn't involve too heavy a cost to the taxpayer. But that would be the case here; and therefore I . . . no, I'm damned . . . and please excuse me . . . if I can go along with Doctor Stockmann this time. Sometimes even gold is too expensive; at least that's my opinion.

Vociferous support from all sides.

Hovstad I also feel obliged to set out my position. To begin with this demonstration of Doctor Stockmann's seemed to gain considerable support, and I endorsed it as impartially as I could. But then we realized we'd allowed ourselves to be led astray by an untrue report . . .

Dr Stockmann Untrue . . .!

Hovstad Well then, a not altogether reliable report. The mayor's statement was the proof of this. I hope no one here doubts my liberal convictions; on the larger political questions everyone knows where *The People's Messenger* stands. But I've learned from experienced and discriminating men, that when it comes to purely local issues, a newspaper needs to proceed with a certain caution.

Aslaksen I completely agree with the speaker.

Hovstad And in this particular case it's now quite obvious that public opinion is opposed to Doctor Stockmann. And what is an editor's first and most important duty, gentlemen? Is it not to function in harmony with his readers? Has he not been given as it were a tacit mandate to promote, assiduously and tirelessly, the well-being of his political allies? Or maybe I'm wrong?

Many Voices No, no, no! Hovstad is right!

Hovstad It's cost me a bitter struggle to break with a man in whose house I have in recent days been a frequent guest . . . a man, who to this day has been able to bask in the undivided goodwill of his contemporaries . . . a man whose only . . . or at any rate principal fault, is to seek advice more often from his heart than from his head.

Various Isolated Voices It's true! Hurrah for Doctor Stockmann!

Hovstad However, it's my duty to society to break with him. And it's out of concern that I'm forced to oppose him and, if possible, block him in this disastrous course he's embarked upon; it's out of concern for his family . . .

Dr Stockmann Stick to the water supply and the sewage system!

Hovstad . . . concern for his wife and his unprotected children.

Morten Is that us, Mother?

Mrs Stockmann Ssh!

Aslaksen So, I shall put the mayor's motion to the vote.

Dr Stockmann No need! This evening I've no intention of talking about that obscenity down at the Baths. No; you're going to hear something quite different.

Mayor (*in an undertone*) What's this now?

A Drunk (*over by the exit*) I pay my taxes! So I'm entitled to express my opinion! And I am of the full . . . firm . . . and unmentionable opinion, that . . .

Several Voices Be quiet back there!

Others He's drunk! Throw him out!

The Drunk is ejected.

Dr Stockmann May I speak?

Aslaksen (*ringing his bell*) Doctor Stockmann has the floor!

Dr Stockmann If, a few days ago, anyone had dared to try to gag me the way you have this evening, I would have defended my sacred human rights like a lion! But I don't care about that any more; now I have more important things to talk about.

The crowd moves in closer to him. Morten Kiil arrives among the spectators.

I've thought and brooded a great deal these last few days . . . brooded about so many subjects that in the end my head was bursting with it all . . .

Mayor (*coughs*) Hm . . .!

Dr Stockmann . . . but then it all began to clear; and I could see a series of distinct connections. And that's why I'm here this evening. I'm here to reveal some important truths, my friends! I'm here to share with you a discovery of a quite different magnitude from the trifling matter that our water supply is poisoned and our health spa is built on plague-infected soil.

Many Voices (*shouting*) Don't talk about the Baths! We don't want to know. Nothing about that.

Dr Stockmann I told you I'm here to speak about the important discovery I've made these last few days . . . the discovery that all our spiritual springs are poisoned and that the whole of our society rests on the plague-infected soil of lies.

Bewildered Voices (*in an undertone*) What's he saying?

Mayor What are you insinuating . . .?

Aslaksen (*his hand on the bell*) The speaker will kindly express himself with moderation.

Dr Stockmann I've loved my native town with that special love a man can only feel for his childhood home. I wasn't very old, when I left here, and distance, homesickness and nostalgia cast a brighter glow over the place and the people in it.

Scattered applause and cheering.

So for many years I was stuck up north in a dreadfully remote corner of the world. When I came into contact with some of the people who lived scattered among those crags, I often thought the poor starving creatures would have been better off with a vet than a man like me.

Murmurs in the room.

Billing (*putting down his pen*) Never heard such a bloody . . .!

Hovstad This is an insult to respectable working people!

Dr Stockmann Just hold on a minute! . . . I don't think anyone could accuse me of forgetting my native town while I was up there. I was as broody as a hen on her eggs; and what I hatched . . . was my plan for the Baths.

Applause and protests.

And when at long last, by a happy twist of fate, I was able to come home again . . . well, my friends, I thought that all my wishes had come true. Except I still had one eager, constant, burning wish; to be of service to my community.

Mayor (*gazing upwards*) Strange way to show it . . . hm.

Dr Stockmann And so I went around for a while puffed up with blind happiness. But yesterday morning . . . no, it was the evening before last . . . the scales dropped from my eyes, I was wide awake, and the first thing I saw was the immense stupidity of the authorities . . .

Noise, shouting and laughter. Mrs Stockmann coughs emphatically.

Mayor Mr Chairman!

Aslaksen (*ringing the bell*) By the powers vested in me . . .!

Dr Stockmann It's petty to pull me up on the strength of one word, Mr Aslaksen. All I mean is, I became aware of the immense amount of bungling our leaders had been responsible for at the Baths. I can't stand leaders, for the life of me . . . I've seen far too much of them in my time. They're like goats in a plantation of saplings; they're nothing but trouble; however many twists and turns a free man may perform, they'll block his way . . . and I should like to see them exterminated, like any other vermin . . .

Uproar in the room.

Mayor Mr Chairman, can we allow this type of outburst?

Aslaksen (*his hand on the bell*) Doctor . . .!

Dr Stockmann I can't understand why it's taken me this long to get a really clear image of these people; when after all I've had a perfect example in front of me almost every day here in the town . . . my brother Peter . . . slow on the uptake and mired in prejudice . . .

Laughter, noise and whistle-blowing. Mrs Stockmann sits, coughing away. Aslaksen rings the bell violently. The Drunk has returned.

Drunk Are you referring to me? It's true my name's Pettersen, I admit it; but I'm damned if I . . .

Angry Voices He's drunk, get him out! Throw him out!

He's thrown out again.

Mayor Who is that man?

A Bystander Don't know him, Mr Mayor.

Another He's not from round here.

A Third He's some timber-merchant from . . .

The rest is inaudible.

Aslaksen The man was obviously drunk on Bavarian beer . . . Go on, now, Doctor; but please proceed with moderation.

Dr Stockmann All right, then, my friends, I shall say no more about our leaders. And if you imagine, from what I've been saying, that I'm out for blood from these gentlemen here this evening, then you'd be mistaken . . . very seriously mistaken. Because I cherish the consoling certainty that these leftovers, all these relics of a dying philosophy, are very well employed digging their own graves; they don't need a doctor's help to hasten their demise. And in any case, they're not really the ones who constitute the greatest danger to society; they're not the ones who are most actively poisoning our spiritual springs or infecting the soil beneath us; they're not the ones who are the most dangerous enemies of truth and freedom in our society.

Voices (*shouting from all corners*) Who is, then? Go on, tell us! Give us the names!

Dr Stockmann Yes, rest assured, I will give you the names! Because the important discovery I made yesterday is precisely this: (*He raises his voice.*) the most dangerous enemy of truth and freedom in our midst is the solid majority. That's right, the damned, solid, liberal majority

. . . that's who it is! And now you know.

Immense noise in the room. Most people are yelling,
stamping and blowing whistles. Several elderly gentle-
men exchange secret glances, apparently enjoying them-
selves. Mrs Stockmann gets up nervously; Ejlif and
Morten approach those schoolchildren who are creating
a disturbance and threaten them. Aslaksen rings the bell
and calls for order. Hovstad and Billing are both speak-
ing, inaudibly. Finally, silence falls.

Aslaksen As chairman, I call on the speaker to retract his
ill-considered outburst.

Dr Stockmann Not on your life, Mr Aslaksen. It's the
vast majority in this society which is depriving me of my
freedom and trying to prevent me from speaking the
truth.

Hovstad The majority always has right on its side.

Billing And bloody truth as well!

Dr Stockmann The majority never has right on its side. I
said never! That's one of those social lies, which a free,
intelligent man has to rebel against. Who is it who makes
up the majority of inhabitants of any given country? The
clever or the stupid? I think we can all agree that all over
the world, the stupid are in a quite frighteningly over-
whelming majority. But surely to God it can't be right that
through all eternity the stupid shall have dominion over
the clever!

Noise and shouting.

Yes, yes; you can shout me down; but you can't deny it.
The majority has the power . . . unfortunately . . . ; but it
doesn't make them *right*. I'm the one who's right, I and one
or two others: individuals. The minority is always right.

Once again, uproar.

Hovstad Ha ha; since yesterday Doctor Stockmann's joined the aristocracy!

Dr Stockmann I've said before that I don't want to waste a word on the small-minded, constricted herd left panting in my wake. They're no longer in touch with the beating heart of life. I'm thinking about the few, those individuals among us who have taken all those young, burgeoning truths and made them our own. These people are, if you like, out manning the outposts so far in advance of the lines that the solid majority are still far behind . . . and they're fighting for truths which are still too newly minted in the general consciousness to have won themselves a majority.

Hovstad And now the doctor's turned revolutionary!

Dr Stockmann Yes, damn it, Mr Hovstad, I have! I intend to stir up a revolution against the lie that the majority is the keeper of the truth. What sort of truths do the majority usually embrace? Truths that are so decrepit, they're on the way to being senile. And when a truth has lasted that long, gentlemen, it's well on the way to being a lie.

Laughter and expressions of scorn.

Yes, yes, think whatever you like about me; but truths are not the rugged old Methuselahs people imagine them to be. An averagely constructed truth lasts . . . let me see . . . seventeen or eighteen years as a rule, twenty years at the most; hardly ever longer. And truths as ancient as that are always dreadfully threadbare. All the same, it's only then the majority gets involved with them and starts recommending them to society as healthy spiritual nourishment. But there's not much nutritional value in that sort of diet, I can assure you; that's one thing, as a doctor, I understand. All these truths for the majority are like last year's condemned meat; they're like rancid, tainted, green salted ham. And they're the source of all the moral scurvy raging through our society.

Aslaksen It's my impression that our distinguished speaker is straying a long way from his text.

Mayor I must by and large second the chairman's point.

Dr Stockmann No, Peter, I think you must have taken leave of your senses. I'm sticking to my text as closely as I can. Because what I want to say is precisely that the masses, the majority, this damned solid majority . . . I'm telling you, that's what's poisoning our spiritual springs and infecting the soil beneath us.

Hovstad And the great liberal majority of the people is acting this way because it's discriminating enough to subscribe to nothing but established and acknowledged truths?

Dr Stockmann Oh, my dear Mr Hovstad, don't talk about established truths! The truths acknowledged by the masses are the truths, which in the days of our grandfathers, only those warriors manning the outposts held to be established. Those of us who man the outposts today no longer acknowledge them; and I think there's only one established truth: that no society can lead a healthy life based on truths so old, the marrow has been sucked out of them.

Hovstad Rather than all this hot air, it might be amusing to hear what are these old truths that have had the marrow sucked out of them.

Support from several quarters.

Dr Stockmann Oh, I could run up a huge list of these tattered beliefs; but to start with I'll confine myself to one acknowledged truth which is actually an ugly lie, but which nevertheless Mr Hovstad and *The People's Messenger* and all *The Messenger*'s supporters live by.

Hovstad And that is . . .?

Dr Stockmann It's the doctrine you've inherited from your forefathers and which you mindlessly proclaim in all directions . . . that the working classes, the mob, the masses are the backbone of the people . . . that they're the people itself . . . and that the common people, people who are ignorant and immature members of society, have the same right to condemn and approve, to govern and advise as the individual, the spiritually superior personality.

Billing Never heard such a bloody . . .!

Hovstad (*at the same time, shouting*) Citizens, you pay attention to this!

Enraged Voices Ha, we're the people, aren't we? So it's only superior people who can govern!

A Worker Don't let him stand there saying things like that, throw him out!

Others Yes, throw him out!

A Citizen (*yelling*) Blow your horn, Evensen!

Mighty blasts on the horn are heard; whistle-blowing and furious noise throughout.

Dr Stockmann (*once the noise has died down somewhat*) Just be reasonable! Can't you bear to listen to the voice of truth for once in a while? It's not as if I'm asking you all to agree with me just like that. But I certainly expected Mr Hovstad to accept what I'm saying, once he'd had a chance to make a slight recovery. Mr Hovstad claims to be a free-thinker . . .

Several Citizens (*in subdued but startled voices*) Did he

94

say free-thinker? What? Is Hovstad a free-thinker?

Hovstad (*shouting*) Prove it, Doctor Stockmann! When have I ever said such a thing in print?

Dr Stockmann (*after a moment's reflection*) No, damn it, you're right; . . . you've never had the courage. Well, I don't want to put you on the rack, Mr Hovstad. Let me be the free-thinker. Let me prove to you all with an illustration from nature how *The People's Messenger* is shamelessly leading you by the nose, when it assures you that you, the working classes, the masses, are the true backbone of the people. Don't you see, it's just a newspaper lie! The working classes are nothing but the raw material, from which a people will be fashioned.

Murmuring, laughter and unrest in the room.

Yes, isn't that how it goes for all the other species in the world? In the animal kingdom, what's the difference between breeding and lack of breeding? Let's take the common barnyard hen. What's the value of the meat on some stunted chicken carcass? Not very much! And what kind of eggs does it lay? Any respectable crow or raven can produce eggs almost as good. And then take a well-bred Spanish or Japanese hen, or a superior pheasant or turkey . . . yes, then you'll see the difference! Or what about dogs, with which we humans have such close relationships? First imagine a simple, common-or-garden dog . . . I mean one of those disgusting, ratty, vulgar mongrels which mooches around the streets lifting its leg against your house. And then compare the mongrel with a pedigree dog, bred through several generations in a superior house, eating fine food and exposed to the sound of harmonious voices and music. Don't you suppose the pedigree's skull is quite differently evolved from the mongrel's? That's right, you can bank on it! It's pedigree puppies like that which the magicians train to perform the

95

most extraordinary tricks. The sort of thing a common barnyard mongrel could never learn, if you stood it on its head.

Noise and laughter spread.

A Citizen (*shouting*) So we're dogs now, are we?

Another Man We're not animals, Doctor!

Dr Stockmann Yes, my friend, by my soul, yes, we are animals! We're as much animals, every one of us, as anyone could ask. But there aren't many superior animals to be found among us. Oh, there's a quite terrifying gap between the poodle men and the pariah men. And the strange thing is that Mr Hovstad completely agrees with me as long as we're talking about four-legged animals . . .

Hovstad Yes, as far as they're concerned.

Dr Stockmann Right; but as soon as I extend this law to cover two-legged animals, Mr Hovstad shuts up like a clam; he no longer dares to have his own opinions or to think his own thoughts to their logical conclusion: he turns the whole doctrine on its head and proclaims in *The Messenger* that the barnyard hen and the street pariah . . . that they're the finest specimens in the whole menagerie. And it'll always be that way, as long as the common element weighs us down and as long as we refuse to work towards spiritual superiority.

Hovstad I make no claim to any kind of superiority. I come from simple peasant stock; and I'm proud that my roots reach deep down into those working people who are being sneered at here.

Many Workers Hurrah for Hovstad! Hurrah, hurrah!

Dr Stockmann The kind of commonness I'm talking about isn't only found deep down; it creeps and swarms

all around us . . . all the way up to the heights of society.
Just look at your own fine, handsome mayor! My brother
Peter is as common a man as anyone on two feet . . .

Laughter and hisses.

Mayor I object to this kind of personal remark.

Dr Stockmann (*imperturbable*) . . . and not because he, as I
am myself, is descended from some old disreputable pirate
from Pomerania or thereabouts . . . yes, that's right . . .

Mayor Ridiculous rumour, I deny it!

Dr Stockmann . . . but because he thinks his employer's
thoughts and shares his employer's opinions. People who
do that are, in a spiritual sense, the common herd; and
that's why my impressive brother Peter is actually so
dreadfully lacking in superior qualities . . . and consequently also so far from liberal.

Mayor Mr Chairman . . .!

Hovstad So in this country superior people are the same
as liberals? That is a completely new discovery.

Laughter in the crowd.

Dr Stockmann Yes, that's also part of my new discovery.
And something else I've discovered is this: that liberalism
is almost exactly the same as morality. And that's why I
say it's absolutely irresponsible of *The Messenger* to proclaim, day in and day out, the false doctrine that it's the
masses, the solid majority, which has commandeered liberalism and morality . . . and that vice and corruption and
every kind of spiritual obscenity are evils which seep out
of culture, like all the filth which seeps down to the Baths
from the tanneries in the valley where the mills are!

Noise and interruptions.

(*imperturbable, laughing in his eagerness*) And yet this same *People's Messenger* can preach that the masses must be raised up to higher standards of living! But, damn it to hell . . . if *The Messenger*'s reasoning is valid, then to raise up the masses would be precisely the same as plunging them straight down into corruption! Fortunately it's only an old lie handed down to the people, this idea that culture is a demoralizing force. On the contrary, what causes this damned situation is stultification, poverty and ugliness in every aspect of life! In a house which is not aired and swept every day . . . ; my wife Katrine maintains that the floors should be scrubbed as well; but that's debatable; . . . anyway . . . in a house like this, in my view, within two or three years, people will lose the ability to think or act morally. A lack of oxygen weakens the conscience. And in many, many houses in this town there seems to be a serious shortage of oxygen, since the whole of the solid majority can mislay its conscience to the extent of wanting to build the town's future on a quagmire of lies and deceit.

Aslaksen I cannot allow such a gross accusation to be flung in the face of an entire community.

A Gentleman I move the chairman order the speaker to be silent.

Emphatic Voices Yes, yes! That's right! Order him to be silent!

Dr Stockmann (*flaring up*) Then I shall shout the truth from every street corner! I shall write for newspapers in other towns! The whole country will know what's being done here!

Hovstad It almost seems as if the doctor intends to destroy the town.

Dr Stockmann Yes, I am so devoted to my native town, I

would rather destroy it than see it flourish on the back of a lie.

Aslaksen Well, now we know.

Noise and whistle-blowing. Mrs Stockmann coughs in vain; the doctor can't hear her any more.

Hovstad (*shouting through the noise*) A man who wants to destroy a whole society must be an enemy to everyone in it.

Dr Stockmann (*increasingly excited*) What does it matter if a society founded on lies is destroyed? I say it ought to be levelled! Everyone who lives by a lie should be exterminated like vermin! You'll end by poisoning the whole country; you'll bring things to a point where the whole country deserves to be laid to waste. And if it comes to that, then I say with all my heart: let the whole country be laid to waste; let everyone in it be exterminated!

A Man (*in the crowd*) He talks like a real enemy of the people!

Billing Bloody right, the voice of the people!

The Whole Crowd Yes, yes, yes! He's an enemy of the people! He hates his country! He hates the whole people!

Aslaksen Both as a citizen and as a human being, I am deeply disturbed by what I've been forced to listen to here. Doctor Stockmann has revealed himself in a way I could never have imagined. Unfortunately, I have to support the opinion just expressed by various deserving citizens; and I suggest that we embody this opinion in a resolution. I propose the following motion: 'This meeting declares that it considers the Medical Officer at the Baths, Doctor Tomas Stockmann, to be an enemy of the people.'

Rousing cheers and applause. A good many people

form a circle round the doctor and blow whistles at him. Mrs Stockmann and Petra have stood up. Morten and Ejlif fight with other schoolchildren, who have also been whistling. A number of adults separate them.

Dr Stockmann (*to the whistle-blowers*) Oh, you idiots, yes, you are . . . I'm telling you . . .

Aslaksen (*ringing the bell*) The doctor is no longer allowed to speak. We should proceed to a formal vote; but in order to spare personal feelings, it should be in writing and anonymous. Do you have some blank paper, Mr Billing?

Billing I have blue paper and white paper . . .

Aslaksen (*stepping down*) Excellent; that should speed things up. Cut it up in pieces . . . ; that's right, yes. (*to the crowd*) Blue means no; white means yes. I shall circulate and collect the votes myself.

The mayor leaves the room. Aslaksen and a couple of other citizens circulate around the meeting, distributing pieces of paper from hats.

1st Gentleman (*to Hovstad*) What's the matter with the doctor? What are we to think?

Hovstad You know how excitable he is.

2nd Gentleman (*to Billing*) Listen; you go to his house.

1st Gentleman Have you noticed if he drinks?

Billing I don't know what to bloody say. The toddy's always on the table, when they have company.

3rd Gentleman No, I just think he's gone off his head.

1st Gentleman Perhaps there's some hereditary insanity in the family?

Billing God, I shouldn't wonder.

4th Gentleman No, this is pure malice; must be some sort of revenge.

Billing He did mention a salary increase the other day; which he didn't get.

All the Gentlemen Oh, well, then; that explains everything!

The Drunk (*in the crowd*) I want a blue one, give me a blue one! And a white one, I want a white one!

Shouts It's that drunk again! Throw him out!

Morten Kiil (*approaching the doctor*) Well, Stockmann, now do you see what comes of pulling these monkey tricks?

Dr Stockmann I've done my duty.

Morten Kiil What were you saying about the tanneries in the valley?

Dr Stockmann You heard; I said that's where all that muck comes from.

Morten Kiil From *my* tannery as well?

Dr Stockmann Unfortunately, your tannery is the worst of the lot.

Morten Kiil Are you going to print that in the paper?

Dr Stockmann I don't intend to hide anything.

Morten Kiil This could cost you dear, Stockmann.

He leaves. A fat gentleman goes up to Horster, ignoring the ladies.

Fat Gentleman So, Captain, you loan out your property to enemies of the people?

Horster I think I can do what I like with my property, Mr Vik.

Fat Gentleman Then you won't mind if I do the same with mine.

Horster What do you mean, Mr Vik?

Fat Gentleman You'll hear from me in the morning. (*He turns and leaves.*)

Petra Wasn't that the owner of your ship, Horster?

Horster Yes, that was Mr Vik.

Aslaksen, with the ballot papers in his hand, steps up on to the dais and rings the bell.

Aslaksen Gentlemen, may I announce to you the result of the vote? Unanimously, with the exception of one vote . . .

A Young Gentleman That was the drunk's!

Aslaksen Unanimously, with the exception of one intoxicated man, this meeting has declared the Medical Officer at the Baths, Doctor Tomas Stockmann, an enemy of the people.

Shouts and bursts of applause.

Long live our old and honourable community!

More applause.

Long live our capable and energetic mayor, who has so loyally suppressed the demands of blood!

Cheers.

I declare the meeting closed. (*He steps down.*)

Billing Long live the chairman!

The Entire Crowd Hurrah for Aslaksen!

Dr Stockmann My hat and my coat, Petra! Captain, do you have room for passengers on your trip to the new world?

Horster We'll find room for you and yours, Doctor.

Dr Stockmann (*as Petra helps him on with his coat*) Good. Come along, Katrine! Come on, boys! (*He takes his wife's arm.*)

Mrs Stockmann (*quietly*) Tomas darling, let's slip out the back way.

Dr Stockmann No back ways, Katrine. (*He raises his voice.*) You're going to hear from this enemy of the people, before he shakes the dust from his feet. I am not as good-natured as a certain person; I'm not going to say: I forgive you; for you know not what you do.

Aslaksen (*shouting*) That is a blasphemous comparison, Doctor Stockmann!

Billing Bloo . . . that's right . . . a serious man shouldn't have to listen to that kind of thing.

A Coarse Voice And he makes threats as well!

Excited Cries Let's smash his windows! Throw him in the fjord!

A Man (*in the crowd*) Blow your horn, Evensen! Toot, toot!

Blasts on the horn, whistle-blowing and wild shouting. The doctor and his family move towards the exit. Horster clears a way for them. The whole crowd yells after them, as they leave.

Crowd Enemy of the people! Enemy of the people! Enemy of the people!

Billing (*organizing his notes*) No bloody toddy at the Stockmanns' house tonight!

The crowd swarms towards the exits; the noise spreads around the area; out in the streets the cry can be heard: 'Enemy of the people! Enemy of the people!'

Act Five

*Dr Stockmann's study. Bookshelves and cupboards with
various medical displays along the walls. Upstage is the
exit to the hall; downstage left, the door to the living-
room. On the stage-right wall are two windows, every
pane of which has been smashed. In the middle of the
room is the doctor's desk, covered with books and papers.
The room is in disarray. It's morning.*

   *Dr Stockmann, in dressing-gown and slippers and
wearing a skull-cap, is bent over, rummaging about under
one of the cupboards with his umbrella; eventually he
fetches out a stone.*

Dr Stockmann (*speaking through the open door to the
living-room*) Katrine, I've found another one.

Mrs Stockmann (*from the living-room*) Oh, you're bound
to find a good many more.

Dr Stockmann (*adding the stone to a pile on the table*) I
shall preserve these stones as a shrine. Ejlif and Morten
will see them every day, and when they're grown up,
they'll inherit them from me. (*He rummages under one of
the bookshelves.*) Hasn't she . . . whatever the hell she's
called . . . her, the girl . . . hasn't she been for the glazier
yet?

Mrs Stockmann (*coming in*) Yes, but he said he didn't
know if he could manage it today.

Dr Stockmann You'll see, he won't dare come.

Mrs Stockmann No, that's what Randine thought, that
he wouldn't dare because of the neighbours. (*She speaks*

to someone in the living-room.) What is it, Randine? Oh,
I see. (*She exits and comes straight back.*)

Mrs Stockmann There's a letter for you, Tomas.

Dr Stockmann Let's have a look. (*He opens it and reads
it.*) Ah, I see.

Mrs Stockmann Who's it from?

Dr Stockmann From the landlord. He's giving us notice.

Mrs Stockmann Is he really? And he's such a decent
man . . .

Dr Stockmann (*looking at the letter*) He says he doesn't
dare not. He's doing it reluctantly; but he doesn't dare not
. . . for the sake of his fellow-citizens . . . in deference to
public opinion . . . he's dependent on . . . he doesn't dare
give offence to certain influential people . . .

Mrs Stockmann You see what I mean, Tomas.

Dr Stockmann Yes, yes, I see; he's a coward, like everyone else in this town; nobody dares do anything in deference to everybody else. (*He throws the letter on to the
table.*) But it's all the same to us, Katrine. We're going to
the new world, and then we'll . . .

Mrs Stockmann Yes, but Tomas, have you really thought
it through, this trip?

Dr Stockmann Maybe I should stay here, where I've been
sat in the stocks as an enemy of the people, branded and
had my windows broken! And look at this, Katrine;
they've torn a hole in my black trousers.

Mrs Stockmann Oh, no; and they're your best!

Dr Stockmann If you go out to fight for freedom and
truth, you should never wear your best trousers. Actually,
I don't really care about trousers, you know; you can

always sew them up for me. But the fact that the masses, the mob, had the temerity to lay hands on me as if they were my equals ... *that's* what I can't take in, for the life of me.

Mrs Stockmann Yes, they've been really vile to you here in the town, Tomas; but does it mean we have to leave the country altogether?

Dr Stockmann Do you think the rabble in our other towns is any less insolent than it is here? No, listen, it'd be much the same wherever you went. Well, never mind; let the mongrels bark; that's not the worst that can happen; the worst thing is that everyone, all over this country, is a slave to some party. Not that ... maybe it's no better in the free West either; perhaps the solid majority and liberal public opinion and all the other infernal trappings flourish over there as well. But there it's on a grander scale, you see; they can kill you, but they don't torture you; they don't squeeze a free spirit in a vice like they do here at home. And if need be you can keep yourself out of things altogether. (*He paces up and down.*) If only I knew of a stretch of jungle or a little South Sea island for sale at a reasonable price ...

Mrs Stockmann Yes, but what about the boys, Tomas?

Dr Stockmann (*stopping*) You're very strange, Katrine! Do you really want the boys to grow up in a society like ours? You saw for yourself yesterday evening that half the population is raving mad; and if the other half hasn't lost its mind, it's only because they're complete blockheads with no minds to lose.

Mrs Stockmann Oh, Tomas darling, you do go in for such wild exaggerations.

Dr Stockmann Ah! You mean it isn't true, what I'm saying? They don't turn every single idea upside down? They don't mix right and wrong up into a fricassee? They don't call everything I know to be true a lie? And the maddest thing of all is that these are grown-up independent people moving round in herds telling themselves and everybody else that they're liberals! Have you ever heard of such a thing, Katrine!

Mrs Stockmann Yes, yes, of course it's mad, but . . .

Petra comes in from the living-room.

Mrs Stockmann You're back early from school.

Petra Yes; I've been fired.

Mrs Stockmann Fired!

Dr Stockmann You as well!

Petra Mrs Busk gave me notice; I thought it was best I leave straight away.

Dr Stockmann You did the right thing, by God!

Mrs Stockmann Who would have thought Mrs Busk could be so horrible!

Petra Oh, mother, she's not horrible; it was quite obvious how much it upset her. But she said she didn't dare do otherwise; and then I was fired.

Dr Stockmann (*laughing and rubbing his hands*) She didn't dare do otherwise, her as well! Oh, isn't it wonderful?

Mrs Stockmann I suppose after yesterday's ugly spectacle . . .

Petra It wasn't just that. Listen to this, father!

Dr Stockmann What?

Petra Mrs Busk showed me no less than three letters she'd received this morning . . .

Dr Stockmann Anonymous no doubt?

Petra Yes.

Dr Stockmann Because they don't dare sign their names, Katrine!

Petra And two of them said that somebody, who was a regular visitor to the house, had said in the club last night that I was so much a free-thinker on a variety of subjects . . .

Dr Stockmann And I'm sure you didn't deny it?

Petra No, of course I didn't. Mrs Busk herself is relatively free-thinking, when it's just the two of us; but since this was now generally known about me, she didn't dare keep me on.

Mrs Stockmann Just think . . . someone who's a regular visitor to the house! That's what you get for your hospitality, Tomas.

Dr Stockmann We're not going to live in this pig-sty a moment longer. Pack as quickly as you can, Katrine; let's get out of here, the sooner the better.

Mrs Stockmann Be quiet; I think there's someone in the hall. Go and have a look, Petra.

Petra (*opening the door*) Oh, it's you, Captain Horster. Please come in.

Horster (*from the hall*) Good morning. I thought I'd just look in to see how everything was.

Dr Stockmann (*shaking his hand*) Thank you; that was very kind of you.

Mrs Stockmann And thanks for helping us get through, yesterday evening, Captain Horster.

Petra How did you get back home?

Horster Oh, that was all right; I'm fairly strong; and that lot are mostly nothing but mouth.

Dr Stockmann Yes, it's remarkable, isn't it, this miserable cowardice? Look, I want to show you something! You see, here are all the stones they've thrown at us. Just look at them! My God, there are only about two decent-sized rocks in the whole pile; the rest are nothing but pebbles . . . gravel really. And they all stood out there screaming and shouting they were going to do for me; but when it comes to action . . . action . . . no, there's not much of that in this town.

Horster Just as well for you on this occasion, Doctor.

Dr Stockmann Well, of course. But all the same, it's infuriating; because if it should ever come one day to some serious, national struggle, you'll see, public opinion will be in favour of making a run for it, and the solid majority will be off after it like a flock of sheep, Captain Horster. That's what's so depressing, that's what really pains me deeply . . . Ah, what the hell . . . this is all just stupid. If they say I'm an enemy of the people, then I might as well be an enemy of the people.

Mrs Stockmann You never will be, Tomas.

Dr Stockmann You shouldn't bank on it, Katrine. An ugly turn of phrase can work like a pin puncturing a lung. And this damned expression . . . ; I can't get rid of it; it's fixed itself tight in the pit of my stomach; it's lying there digging and biting like acid. And no milk of magnesia can help.

Petra Hah; you should just laugh at them, Father.

Horster People will change their minds, Doctor.

Mrs Stockmann Yes, Tomas, as sure as you're standing here.

Dr Stockmann Yes, maybe, when it's too late. And much good may it do them! Then they can wallow in their pig-sty and be sorry they drove a patriot into exile. When are you sailing, Captain Horster?

Horster Ah . . . this is the real reason I've come to see you . . .

Dr Stockmann Oh, is there something the matter with the ship?

Horster No; but I'm not going to be on it.

Petra Surely you haven't been fired?

Horster (*smiling*) Yes, actually I have.

Petra You as well.

Mrs Stockmann You see, Tomas.

Dr Stockmann And in the name of truth! Oh, if I'd thought something like this might happen . . .

Horster You mustn't worry about it; I'll soon find a command with another shipping company in some other town.

Dr Stockmann So that's how Vik the shipowner behaves . . . and he's a wealthy man, not dependent on anyone . . .! Well, I'll be damned!

Horster Generally, he's quite a fair-minded man; he said himself he'd like to have kept me on, if only he dared . . .

Dr Stockmann But he didn't dare? Well, of course.

Horster It's not so simple, he said, when you're a member of a party . . .

Dr Stockmann A true word from a man of honour! A party's like a mincing machine; it grinds everyone's head to mince; and from then on they're all meatheads, all in one stew.

Mrs Stockmann Really, Tomas!

Petra (*to Horster*) If only you hadn't escorted us home, perhaps this wouldn't have happened.

Horster I have no regrets.

Petra (*reaching out her hand to him*) Thank you!

Horster (*to the doctor*) I wanted to tell you, if you really do want to leave, I've had another idea . . .

Dr Stockmann Well, good; as long as we can get away quickly . . .

Mrs Stockmann Ssh; wasn't that somebody knocking?

Petra I bet it's uncle.

Dr Stockmann Aha. (*shouting*) Come in!

Mrs Stockmann Tomas darling, please promise me . . .

The mayor comes in from the hall.

Mayor (*in the doorway*) Oh, you're busy. Then I'd rather . . .

Dr Stockmann No, no; come in.

Mayor But I wanted a private word.

Mrs Stockmann We'll go and sit in the living-room.

Horster And I'll call again later.

Dr Stockmann No, stay with them, Captain Horster; I want to ask you something else . . .

Horster All right, then, I'll wait.

He follows Mrs Stockmann and Petra into the living-room. The mayor says nothing, but glances at the windows.

Dr Stockmann Perhaps you find it a bit draughty today? I should put your cap on.

Mayor Thanks, maybe I will. (*He does so.*) I think I might have caught cold last night; I was freezing . . .

Dr Stockmann Really? I thought it was quite warm enough.

Mayor I'm sorry it wasn't in my power yesterday to curb those excesses.

Dr Stockmann Have you anything particular to say?

Mayor (*taking out a large letter*) I have to give you this document from the Board at the Baths.

Dr Stockmann My dismissal?

Mayor Yes, effective from today. (*He puts the letter down on the table.*) We regret this; but . . . to be blunt . . . we didn't dare do otherwise in view of public opinion.

Dr Stockmann (*smiling*) Didn't dare? Haven't I heard that somewhere before today?

Mayor I want you to be quite clear about your position. From now on, you mustn't expect to be able to keep up your practice in this town.

Dr Stockmann To hell with my practice! But what makes you so sure?

Mayor The Property-owners' Association has drawn up a petition which it's taking from door to door. All right-minded citizens are requested not to make use of your services; and I daresay not a single householder will refuse to sign; they quite simply wouldn't dare.

Dr Stockmann No, no; I'm sure you're right. And then what?

Mayor If I might offer you some advice, I should move away from here for a while . . .

Dr Stockmann Yes, in fact, I was considering moving away.

Mayor Good. And when you've had six months or so to think about things, and after mature consideration you can bring yourself to write a few apologetic words admitting your mistake . . .

Dr Stockmann Then I might be able to get my post back, you mean?

Mayor Perhaps; it's certainly not impossible.

Dr Stockmann Ah, but what about public opinion? Surely you wouldn't dare, in view of public opinion.

Mayor Opinion is an extremely variable matter. And, to be honest, to have such a written admission from you is very important to us.

Dr Stockmann Oh, so that's what you're after, is it? But don't you remember, damn it, what I said to you before about these kinds of dirty tricks?

Mayor At that time you were in a much more favourable position; at that time you were bold enough to suppose you had the whole town behind you . . .

Dr Stockmann Yes, and now I feel I have the whole town on top of me . . . (*He flares up*.) But no, even if I had the devil himself and his grandmother on top of me . . .! Never . . . I'm telling you, never!

Mayor A man with a family to provide for doesn't dare to behave like this. You don't dare, Tomas.

Dr Stockmann Don't dare? There's only one thing in the world a free man doesn't dare do; and do you know what that is?

Mayor No.

Dr Stockmann Of course you don't; so let me tell you. A free man doesn't dare foul himself like a derelict; he doesn't dare behave in such a way that he'd be forced to spit in his own face!

Mayor This all sounds very plausible; and if there were no other explanation for your stubbornness . . . ; but of course there is . . .

Dr Stockmann What are you talking about?

Mayor I'm sure you understand me very well. But as your brother and as someone with a bit of sense, I advise you not to put too much trust in hopes and projects, which might very easily go wrong.

Dr Stockmann But what on earth is that supposed to mean?

Mayor Are you really trying to tell me you don't know what arrangements Mr Kiil has made in his will?

Dr Stockmann I know that the little he has is going to a foundation for old and destitute manual workers. What's that got to do with me?

Mayor To start with, we're not talking about a little here. Mr Kiil is a comparatively wealthy man.

Dr Stockmann I never had any idea he . . .!

Mayor Hm . . . really not? So you also never had any idea that a not insignificant share of his fortune is left to your children, with provision for you and your wife to enjoy the interest for life? He's never told you?

Dr Stockmann No, I'm damned if he has! On the contrary; he never stops grumbling about how unreasonably high his taxes are. But are you quite certain about this, Peter?

Mayor I have it from a thoroughly reliable source.

Dr Stockmann Well, my God, so Katrine will be secure ... and the children as well! I must tell her right away ... (*shouting*) Katrine, Katrine!

Mayor (*trying to restrain him*) Ssh, don't say anything yet!

Mrs Stockmann (*opening the door*) What's going on?

Dr Stockmann Nothing; go back in.

Mrs Stockmann closes the door. Dr Stockmann paces up and down.

Secure! Just think ... they'll all be secure! For life! It's a wonderful feeling to know you're secure!

Mayor Yes, but that's exactly what you can't say. Mr Kiil can annul the will any time he feels like it.

Dr Stockmann But, my dear Peter, he's not going to do that. The Badger is deliriously happy that I've stood up to you and your high and mighty friends.

Mayor (*starting and looking searchingly at him*) Ah, that explains a lot.

Dr Stockmann Does it?

Mayor So the whole thing was an orchestrated manoeuvre. These violent, reckless attacks you've launched ... in the name of truth ... against the town's leaders ...

Dr Stockmann Well, what about them?

Mayor They were nothing but the arranged price for that vindictive old man Morten Kiil's will.

Dr Stockmann (*almost speechless*) Peter . . . you're the most despicable scum I've ever known in all my life.

Mayor It's finished between us. Your dismissal is irrevocable; . . . and now we have a weapon against you. (*He exits.*)

Dr Stockmann Shame on you, shame, shame! (*shouting*) Katrine! The floor's going to have to be scrubbed where he's been standing! Tell her to bring in the bucket, her . . her . . . what the hell's her . . . her, the one who's always got soot on her nose . . .

Mrs Stockmann (*in the living-room doorway*) Ssh, ssh, Tomas!

Petra (*also in the doorway*) Father, grandpa's here, he wants to know if he can have a word with you alone.

Dr Stockmann Yes, of course he can. (*at the door*) Come in, Mr Kiil.

Morten Kiil comes in. The doctor closes the door behind him.

Well, what can I do for you? Sit down.

Morten Kiil I'll stand. (*He looks around.*) Your house is in a nice state today, Stockmann.

Dr Stockmann Yes, it is, isn't it?

Morten Kiil A very nice state; and fresh air as well; certainly enough of that oxygen you were going on about yesterday. Your conscience must be in very good order today, I imagine.

Dr Stockmann Yes, it is.

Morten Kiil I can imagine. (*He taps his chest.*) But do you know what I have here?

Dr Stockmann A conscience in equally good order, I hope.

Morten Kiil Hah! Something much better than that.

He takes out a thick wallet and opens it, displaying some papers. Dr Stockmann looks at him in amazement.

Dr Stockmann Shares in the Baths?

Morten Kiil Not too difficult to get hold of today.

Dr Stockmann And you've been out buying . . .?

Morten Kiil As many as I could afford.

Dr Stockmann But, my dear Mr Kiil . . . with the Baths in such a desperate state . . .

Morten Kiil If you behave like a reasonable man, you'll get the Baths up and running again.

Dr Stockmann Well, as you've seen for yourself, I'm doing everything I can; but . . . everyone in this town is mad!

Morten Kiil Yesterday you said the worst muck came from my tannery. Well, if that's true, my grandfather and my father before me and I myself must have been polluting the town for all these years, like three avenging angels. Do you think I'm going to take these accusations lying down?

Dr Stockmann I'm afraid you'll probably have to.

Morten Kiil No thanks. I'm going to preserve my good name and my reputation. I've heard it said, people call me 'the Badger'. A badger is a kind of pig, isn't it; they've got no right to call me that. I want to live and die with my name clean.

Dr Stockmann And how are you going to manage that?

Morten Kiil You're going to clean my name for me, Stockmann.

Dr Stockmann Me!

Morten Kiil Do you know what money I used to buy those shares? No, how could you; but I'm going to tell you now. It's the money I've left to Katrine and Petra and the boys. Yes, you see, I have been able to put a little bit by, after all.

Dr Stockmann (*flaring up*) And you've gone and spent Katrine's money on something like that!

Morten Kiil Yes, all the money is now invested in the Baths. And now I want to see whether you really are stark . . . staring . . . mad after all, Stockmann. If you go on saying those animals and all that sort of filth come down from my tannery, it'll be exactly the same as if you're peeling great strips of skin off Katrine and Petra and the boys; and no decent family man would do a thing like that . . . not unless he was a lunatic.

Dr Stockmann (*pacing up and down*) Yes, but I am a lunatic; I am a lunatic!

Morten Kiil You can't be that raving mad, when it concerns your wife and children.

Dr Stockmann (*stopping in front of him*) Why couldn't you have spoken to me, before you went and bought all that waste paper?

Morten Kiil What's done is done.

Dr Stockmann (*moving around restlessly*) If only I wasn't so certain of my case . . .! But I'm completely convinced I'm right.

Morten Kiil (*weighing the wallet in his hand*) If you persist with this madness, then these aren't going to be worth a great deal. (*He puts the wallet back in his pocket.*)

Dr Stockmann Listen, damn it, surely science is going to be able to come up with some sort of antidote, I'd have thought; some sort of prophylactic . . .

Morten Kiil You mean to kill off these animals?

Dr Stockmann Yes, or make them harmless.

Morten Kiil Why don't you try some rat poison?

Dr Stockmann Oh, don't talk rubbish! . . . The thing is, at the moment, everyone's saying I've imagined the whole thing. Well, maybe it is all imaginary! Let them have it their way! The ignorant, narrow-minded mongrels accused me of being an enemy of the people; . . . and they were ready to rip the clothes off my back!

Morten Kiil And break all your windows!

Dr Stockmann Yes, and a man does have a duty to his family! I must talk to Katrine; she'll know what to do.

Morten Kiil That's right; just listen to the advice of a sensible woman.

Dr Stockmann (*bearing down on him*) How could you behave so irresponsibly? To gamble with Katrine's money; to put me in this dreadful, painful position! When I look at you, it's as if I'm looking at the devil himself . . .!

Morten Kiil Then I'll go. But I need an answer from you by two o'clock. Yes or no. If it's no, the shares will go to my foundation . . . today as ever is.

Dr Stockmann And then what will Katrine get?

Morten Kiil Not a penny.

The door to the hall is opened. Hovstad and Aslaksen appear.

Well, look who's here!

Dr Stockmann (*staring at them*) What! You have the nerve to come to my house!

Hovstad We certainly do.

Aslaksen You see, there's something we need to discuss with you.

Morten Kiil (*whispering*) Yes or no . . . by two o'clock.

Aslaksen (*glancing at Hovstad*) Aha!

Morten Kiil exits.

Dr Stockmann Now, what do you want from me? Keep it short.

Hovstad I can understand you're angry with us after the position we took at the meeting yesterday . . .

Dr Stockmann Call that a position? Wonderful position, wasn't it? Faint-hearted, I call it, old-womanish . . . a damned disgrace!

Hovstad Call it what you like; we had no choice.

Dr Stockmann You didn't dare do otherwise? Is that it?

Hovstad If you like.

Aslaksen But why didn't you give us a hint in advance? Just some sort of sign to Mr Hovstad or me.

Dr Stockmann Sign? What about?

Aslaksen About what was behind it.

Dr Stockmann I don't understand what you're talking about.

Aslaksen (*nodding confidentially*) Oh, yes, you do, Doctor Stockmann.

Hovstad You don't have to go on keeping it secret.

Dr Stockmann (*looking from one to the other*) What the hell's . . .?

Aslaksen May I ask . . . is your father-in-law not going round town buying up shares in the Baths?

Dr Stockmann Yes, he's been out buying shares today; but . . .?

Aslaksen Might have been cleverer to get someone else to do it . . . someone not quite so close to you.

Hovstad And you shouldn't have come forward under your own name. Nobody needed to know the attack on the Baths came from you. You should have consulted me, Doctor Stockmann.

Dr Stockmann stares straight ahead of him; then a light seems to dawn on him.

Dr Stockmann (*thunderstruck*) Is this conceivable? Is it possible?

Aslaksen (*smiling*) Well, it's obviously possible. But it needs a little more subtlety, you see.

Hovstad And it needs a few more accomplices; to bring in others always reduces the risk for the individual.

Dr Stockmann (*calmly*) Come to the point, gentlemen . . . what do you want?

Aslaksen Mr Hovstad is probably best . . .

Hovstad No, you say it, Aslaksen.

Aslaksen All right, the thing is, now we understand the background to this whole thing, we've decided we can risk putting *The People's Messenger* at your disposal.

Dr Stockmann *Now* you can risk it? But what about public opinion? Aren't you afraid of raising a storm of protest?

Hovstad We can ride out a storm.

Aslaksen But I'm sure you'll appreciate, Doctor, you'll have to move quickly. And once your attack has served its purpose . . .

Dr Stockmann You mean, once my father-in-law and I have got our hands on all those cheap shares . . .?

Hovstad It's no doubt scientific considerations which are driving you to take control of the Baths yourself.

Dr Stockmann Naturally; and it was scientific considerations which prompted me to bring old Badger in on this. And then we patch up the water system a bit and root around a bit on the beach, and it doesn't cost the ratepayers a single thing. That should work, shouldn't it? What do you think?

Hovstad I think . . . with *The People's Messenger* behind you . . .

Aslaksen In a free society, Doctor, the press is very powerful.

Dr Stockmann Yes; and then there's public opinion; and the Property-owners' Association, Mr Aslaksen, do you think you can deliver them?

Aslaksen The Property-owners' Association and the Temperance Society. Don't worry about that.

Dr Stockmann But, gentlemen . . . ; I'm almost ashamed to ask; but . . . what sort of a fee . . .?

Hovstad Naturally we'd prefer to help you for nothing.

But *The Messenger*'s on a very shaky footing; it's not really taking off; and in the paper's present position, when there's so much to work for in a wider political context, I'd really hate to have to close it down.

Dr Stockmann Of course; it must be very difficult for a friend of the people like yourself. (*flaring up*) But I'm an enemy of the people, aren't I! (*He strides around the room.*) Where's my stick? Where the hell is my stick?

Hovstad What do you mean?

Aslaksen You're not thinking of . . .?

Dr Stockmann (*stopping*) And suppose when I'd sold all my shares, I refused to give you a single penny? Don't forget we rich people can be pretty tight-fisted.

Hovstad And you shouldn't forget this business with the shares is open to more than one interpretation.

Dr Stockmann Yes, I wouldn't put it past you; if I don't come to *The Messenger*'s rescue, then you'll be sure to take a dim view of the whole matter . . . I can imagine, you'll hunt me down . . . pursue me . . . try to throttle me, like the dog throttles the hare!

Hovstad It's the law of nature; survival of the fittest.

Aslaksen You have to take your food where you can find it, you see.

Dr Stockmann Then see if you can find some out in the gutter; (*He strides around the room.*) because now we're damn well going to find out which of us three animals is the fittest. (*He finds an umbrella and starts swinging it.*) Ah, what about this . . .!

Hovstad You're not going to attack us!

Aslaksen Watch what you're doing with that umbrella!

124

Dr Stockmann Out of the window with you, Mr Hovstad!

Hovstad (*at the hall door*) Have you gone mad!

Dr Stockmann Out of the window, Mr Aslaksen! Jump, I tell you! The quicker the better.

Aslaksen (*running round the desk*) Moderation, Doctor; I'm not a strong man; I can't take much . . . (*screaming*) Help, help!

Mrs Stockmann, Petra and Horster come in from the living-room.

Mrs Stockmann God help us, Tomas, what's going on!

Dr Stockmann (*swinging his umbrella*) Jump out, I tell you! Into the gutter!

Hovstad Attacking a defenceless man! I'm calling you as a witness, Captain Horster. (*He rushes out through the hall.*)

Aslaksen (*at a loss*) If I knew my way around . . . (*He slips out through the living-room.*)

Mrs Stockmann (*hanging on to the doctor*) Control yourself, Tomas!

Dr Stockmann (*throwing the umbrella aside*) Damn it, they got away!

Mrs Stockmann But what did they want?

Dr Stockmann I'll explain later; I have other things to think about now. (*He goes to his desk and writes something on a visiting-card.*) Look at this, Katrine; what does this say?

Mrs Stockmann Three big 'NO's; what does that mean?

Dr Stockmann I'll explain that later as well. (*He hands* *over the card.*) There you are, Petra; tell Sooty to run up and give this to Badger, as quick as she can. Hurry up!

Petra takes the card and goes out into the hall.

Well, if I haven't been visited today by all the devil's messengers, then I don't know what. But now I'm going to sharpen my pen against them until it's like a dagger; I'll dip it in poison and gall; I shall throw my inkstand straight at their heads!

Mrs Stockmann Yes, but we're going away, Tomas.

Petra comes back.

Dr Stockmann Well?

Petra Done.

Dr Stockmann Good . . . Did you say going away? No, I'm damned if we are. We're staying right where we are, Katrine!

Petra Staying!

Mrs Stockmann In this town?

Dr Stockmann That's right; this is the battlefield; this is where the fight's going to be; and this is where I shall win the victory! Once I've had my trousers mended, I shall set out round the town and look for a house; we shall need a roof over our heads this winter.

Horster I can offer you that.

Dr Stockmann Can you?

Horster You might as well take it; I have plenty of room and I'm hardly ever there.

Mrs Stockmann That's very kind of you, Horster.

Petra Thank you!

Dr Stockmann (*shaking his hand*) Thank you, thank you! Well, that's one worry less. I'm going to start work right away, today. Oh, Katrine, there's no end to what needs doing! But the good thing is, from now on all my time's my own; yes, you see; now I've been dismissed from the Baths . . .

Mrs Stockmann (*sighing*) Well, I was expecting that.

Dr Stockmann . . . and they're going to take my practice away from me as well. Well, let them! The poor will stay with me anyway . . . the ones who don't pay; and God knows, they're the ones who need me most. But they're going to have to listen to me, damn it; I shall preach to them by day and by night, as it says somewhere.

Mrs Stockmann Tomas darling, I thought you'd already seen what preaching does for you.

Dr Stockmann You're really strange, Katrine. Am I supposed to let myself be beaten down by public opinion and the solid majority and all that viciousness? No thanks. And what I want is so clear and simple and straight-forward. I just want to knock it into those mongrel heads, that liberals are the free man's most devious enemy . . . that the party line will strangle all the liveliest truths at birth . . . and that an obsessive concern for correctness will turn morality and justice on its head, until in the end living here will be really intolerable. Don't you think, Captain Horster, these are subjects I should be able to make people grasp?

Horster Could well be; I don't really understand these things.

Dr Stockmann You see . . . listen to this! The party chiefs have to be exterminated. Because a party chief is like a wolf, you see . . . he's like a ravenous grey wolf . . . he needs so many units of livestock a year, just to keep alive.

Now think about Hovstad and Aslaksen! How many units of livestock do they finish off; or maim or tear to pieces, so they'll never be anything but property-owners or subscribers to *The People's Messenger*! (*He half-sits on the table.*) No, come over here, Katrine . . . look how beautifully the sun shines in today. And all this glorious fresh air that's been let into my room today.

Mrs Stockmann Yes, if we could only live on sunshine and fresh air, Tomas.

Dr Stockmann Oh, you'll have to scrimp and save a bit, that's all . . . that'll be all right. That's the least of my worries. No, the worst thing is I don't know of any free and superior man who'd dare to take up my work after I've gone.

Petra Oh, don't worry about that, father; you've got plenty of time . . . ah, look, here are the boys.

Ejlif and Morten come in from the living-room.

Mrs Stockmann Did they let you out early today?

Morten No; but we were fighting with the others during break . . .

Ejlif That's not true; they were fighting us.

Morten Yes, and so Mr Rørlund said it was best if we stayed at home for a few days.

Dr Stockmann snaps his fingers and jumps down from the table.

Dr Stockmann I've got it! My God, I've got it! You'll never set foot in that school again!

Boys No more school!

Mrs Stockmann But, Tomas . . .

Dr Stockmann Never again! I'll teach you myself . . . means you won't learn a damn thing . . .

Morten Hurrah!

Dr Stockmann . . . but I will turn you into free and superior men . . . And listen, you must help me, Petra.

Petra Yes, Father, I will.

Dr Stockmann And school will be in sight of that place where they called me an enemy of the people. But we must have more pupils; I need at least twelve boys to begin with.

Mrs Stockmann You won't find them in this town.

Dr Stockmann We'll see. (*to the boys*) Do you know any street kids . . . any real urchins . . .?

Morten Yes, Father, lots!

Dr Stockmann Very good; bring some of them in to see me. I'll experiment with some mongrels just this once; sometimes you can find some remarkable specimens.

Morten And what are we going to do, when we've become free and superior men?

Dr Stockmann You're going to hunt the grey wolves and drive them all the way to the far West, boys!

Ejlif looks slightly concerned; Morten jumps up and down and cheers.

Mrs Stockmann Oh, as long as it isn't the grey wolves who are hunting you, Tomas.

Dr Stockmann Have you taken leave of your senses, Katrine! Hunting *me*! When I'm the strongest man in the town!

Mrs Stockmann The strongest . . . now?

Dr Stockmann Yes, I'm not afraid to say it, I'm now one of the strongest men in the whole world.

Morten Gosh!

Dr Stockmann (*lowering his voice*) Ssh; don't tell anyone about it yet, but I've made a great discovery.

Mrs Stockmann Another one?

Dr Stockmann Yes, that's right, that's right! (*He gathers them around him and speaks confidentially.*) The thing is, you see, that the strongest man in the world is the man who stands most alone.

Mrs Stockmann (*smiling and shaking her head*) Oh, Tomas . . .!

Petra (*optimistic, grasping his hand*) Father!